Secrets of a *Sinner*

YOLONDA TONETTE SANDERS

Secrets of a *Sinner*

SECRETS OF A SINNER

A New Spirit Novel

ISBN-13: 978-0-373-83132-6
ISBN-10:   0-373-83132-3

www.kimanipress.com

Printed in U.S.A.

This book is dedicated to anyone being held a prisoner of your past. May you find freedom in Christ.

Acknowledgments

I must first thank God for everything that He's done in my life, for every door that He's opened and the ones that He's closed. If it weren't for Him ordering my steps, this story would not exist or be in your hands. Lord, despite all of my shortcomings, You still found fit to use me. May this book bring much honor and glory to Your Name.

I've heard many times that people come into our lives for a reason, a season or a lifetime, but I didn't always embrace the concept because I usually want to classify those who touch my life in a special way as life-timers. However, I'm learning that sometimes people are assigned to us by God for specific seasons; and when their time is up, we must let them go. To everyone, whether you have been placed in my life for a specific season, a reason, or I'm blessed to have you as a life-timer, I just want to take this time and say "thank you" for your assignment in my life.

To my husband and best friend, David—it has not always been easy, but it has always been worth it. Thank you for loving me through the good and the bad. I love you and I thank God for blessing me with you. You have supported my writing ministry through it all. It would be impossible for me to list the many things that I am grateful to you for—all the scenarios I run by you, the chapters I ask you to proofread, the times you have taken up my slack because I'm writing/traveling, the numerous budget adjustments we've had to make so I could continue to write, and the list goes on…. I know you are proud of me, and I of you as well. I'm especially proud and honored to have the title of being your wife.

To my children, Tre and Tia—you all are a reminder of how blessed I am. I don't take being your mother for granted. You both are very special to me and I love you, I love you, I love you!

To my parents, Wilene Brown and Eddie Brown—I feel like I have the most supportive parents on earth. I love you both. Daddy, thank you for traveling with me and making sure I got to where I needed to be when I was on tour for *Soul Matters*. Ma, thank you for all the times you took off when I was

traveling to come down and help David with the kids.
(I also want to thank Mr. Decker for letting my mama take off,
and Tonya for filling in while she was gone.)

To members of my family (via biology or marriage) and my
friends—I am in awe over the magnitude of support I have
received from you. Many of you have gone above and beyond to
show your love and support of me. I thank and love you all.

To Danella Hicks, Carla Laskey and Janice Sanders—thank you
for all the time you invested in proofreading *Secrets of a Sinner,*
and for the words of encouragement offered along the way.
I love you for once again sticking by my side.

To Tyree Ayers, Michelle (Graham) Jones, Kim Hahn,
Teresa Lewis, Sharon Lindsey and Jennifer Schwind—each of
you contributed to the completion of this novel by reading
sample chapters and helping me work through various scenarios.
To Dr. John N. Singer—thank you for sharing your input, as
well, that day you were in town and stopped by to visit us. I was
knee-deep in the editing process and you helped me simplify
some things. I appreciate all of you. Michelle, I also thank
you for accompanying me on my "field trip" when I had to do
research for one of the scenes.

To Deidre Hampton, John Martin, Willie Marshall,
Peggy Parsely, Robin Thornton, Clarke Tobin, Peter Tobin,
Suzy Tobin and Tonya Turner—thank you all for willingly
and eagerly providing me with information as I was doing
research for this story.

I must apologize because in my acknowledgments for
Soul Matters, I was negligent in that I forgot to include
several key spiritual influences in my life. I want to be sure to
acknowledge you now. I want to thank Elder Latham and Sister
Erma Stowers, and everyone who poured into my life while I
was growing up at New Hope C.O.G.I.C. (Sandusky, OH).
I also want to thank Reverend and Sister Mickles (or as I call
them, "Uncle Sammy" and "Aunt Mildred") of Providence Baptist
Church (Sandusky, OH). I thank all of you for planting seeds of
truth in my life starting at an early age, which I'm certain have
prepared me for this journey. Despite my oversight when writing

acknowledgments for *Soul Matters,* you all were merciful
and continued to show me unconditional love, support
and prayers without ever seeking or asking for recognition.
I thank you for that as well.

To Bishop Timothy J. Clarke, Sister C and my entire
First Church family (Columbus, OH)—I appreciate your love
and support. Bishop Clarke, thank you for watering those
spiritual seeds in my life through your many powerful
and life-changing sermons. God has definitely used you to
speak profound words into my life, and I'm sure the lives of
thousands of others. I pray for His continued blessings
over you and your ministry.

To David Zeyen with the Franklin County Prosecutor's
Office—thank you for patiently answering all of my questions
so thoroughly! I also want to thank Connie Thompson of the
Franklin County Corrections Systems for arranging my
jail tour, Major Strickler for the approval for the tour and
Deputy Scott Spencer for being such a well-informed tour guide.

To my editor, Glenda Howard—you have been a Godsend.
I am thankful for the opportunity to work with you. The things
I've learned from you have helped me to grow as a writer.
You have a sweet spirit and it has been a pleasure to go through
the publishing process with you. To everyone at Kimani Press/
New Spirit and Harlequin who had a hand in producing
Secrets of a Sinner—I don't know all of your names,
but I want you to know that, from the bottom of my heart,
I thank you for all of your hard work and effort. This would
not have happened without you.

To my cousin, LaKesha Raynor—despite the fact that we didn't
start getting to know one another until well after this story
was written, it feels like you have always been part of the
process. Perhaps it's your infectious enthusiasm…or your words
of encouragement…or all the times I've called on you for help
for one reason or another. For all the above and more, I say
"thank you" and "slap it high!" LOL!

To my Faith and Fiction Fellowship tour buddies—
Angela Benson, Mata Elliott, Bonnie Hopkins, LaTonya Mason,
Leslie J. Sherrod and Tiffany L. Warren—I had so much fun
traveling and touring with you all. Thank you for your prayers,
words of encouragement, support, and for putting up with my
crazy behind. May each of you continue to glorify God with
your gift of writing. (To Kym Fisher—you may not have been
on the program, but you were definitely part of our sisterhood.
Thanks for being there for us all!)

To MaRita Teague—it takes a special kind of person to rejoice
over the blessings of others when your own blessing has been
delayed. Thank you for sharing in my joy. Keep standing in
faith and believing that God will reward you.

To *all* authors that I've had the pleasure of meeting since
I've entered the literary world—thank you for welcoming
and accepting me as one of your own.

To all book clubs, organizations, churches, bookstores, print
publications, radio and TV personalities who have supported me
along the way—you all have played a major role in informing
others about my writing projects. Thank you for everything.

To everyone who wrote me, called me or offered prayers
and well-wishes to encourage me along the way—it would be
impossible to list you all by name, but I want to thank you
for blessing me with your words of kindness, encouragement
and prayers.

To everyone who is reading this book—thank you for your
time. I hope this story will not only be entertaining to you, but
a blessing as well.

If I have neglected to mention anyone, please know that my
failing to include your name is a result of my imperfections and
is no indication of how I value your contribution.

Last, but definitely not least, to all the "Natalies" in the world—
I may write about the more "likeable" characters in *Soul Matters*
one day, but this story was pressed upon my heart more than
any other because I wanted to get a clear message through:
God doesn't feel the same way about you as most people do.

He hates your sins, but He doesn't hate *you*. No matter how "bad" your sins may seem compared to the sins of others, in reality, God doesn't weigh sins. Jesus is waiting to forgive you of *all* your sins, just like He forgave me and everyone else who has accepted His gift of salvation. May you say "yes" to Him and experience the kind of love and forgiveness that only He can give.

Love,

Yolonda

www.yolonda.net

Chapter 1

A Way Out

"Excuse me, ma'am—will this be with cash or credit?" The waiter, a short bald, Caucasian who had introduced himself earlier as Paul, walked up to Natalie.

"I don't know," Natalie answered roughly, her narrow, copper-brown eyes peering up at him. Her matching pearl necklace and earrings complemented the black dress she was wearing, which accentuated every curve of her body. Her dark, shoulder-length hair was pinned up and two tiny spiral curls dangled on either side of her honey-colored face. "You'll have to ask my boyfriend. He'll be back—he went to the rest room." Natalie's sharp glance at the waiter silently requested that he leave until her date returned.

"Are you referring to the gentleman who was just in here with you?"

"Yes," she answered, though it seemed like a pretty dumb question. Who else would she be referring to?

Paul frowned, "Ma'am, he left. On the way out, he said you were ready for the bill. Again, will this be cash or credit?"

"What! You have got to be kidding me," Natalie accused. Her eyes roamed back and forth between Paul and the private-dining-room door. She hoped he'd been mistaken. It wasn't her date who'd left the restaurant. It had to be someone else's. Any minute, Kevin would come waltzing through the door and the two of them would work out their issues and go home.

Her eyes were now glued to the door as she drummed her nails on the table, still trying to convince herself that Kevin would be back shortly. He *had* to come back. After all, it had been his idea to eat at this fancy restaurant in the first place. In addition to ordering a very expensive Italian wine, Kevin had ordered three entrées: lobster, steak and chicken, though he'd barely touched any of them. At an upscale establishment like Skyler's, each one of those entrees ranged anywhere from fifty to seventy-five dollars. Sure, he had a right to be upset with her, but he wouldn't walk out without paying the bill...would he?

"Will—this—be—cash—or—credit?" Paul raised his voice, seemingly irritated by Natalie's lack of response. The intensity with which he spoke forced Natalie to accept the truth. Kevin was gone.

Natalie stood up and snatched the bill out of his hands. "Oh my God!" She grabbed the table to keep her tall, slender frame from falling when she saw the total printed in bold, black ink at the bottom. The dinner came to $567.98, including tax, tip and the service charge for using a private room. "I—I—I can't afford this," she stammered.

"You *are* Renée Coleman, correct?"

"Yes," she admitted quietly. The reservation had been made using her middle name.

"Ma'am, I'm sorry but since you made the reservation, *you* are responsible for tonight's meal," he affirmed.

"Wait a minute. There has to be a misunderstanding here." Natalie had less than twenty dollars in her purse, and all of her credit cards were maxed out. Since moving back to Ohio from New York where she'd been pursuing a modeling career, Natalie hadn't worked full-time. She still modeled occasionally and was also registered with a local temporary agency. However, with her mother battling breast cancer and being in and out of the hospital so much, the work assignments that Natalie could accept were few and far between. It was impossible to hold down a full-time job, model on the side and look after her mother all at the same time. "I'll just call Kevin and clarify this whole thing. I'm sure he probably meant to give you his credit card or pay for it before he left," Natalie said to Paul as she nervously got her cell phone out of her purse and dialed Kevin's number.

"Yeah?" Kevin answered the phone in a calm voice.

"Where are you?" Natalie demanded.

"I'm in my car driving on the freeway."

"How dare you leave without telling me? You forgot to pay the bill."

"No, I didn't."

She turned away from the waiter and whispered into the phone, "Kevin, I know you're upset, but this is not the time for games. I don't have any money."

"Aw, I'm sorry to hear that. I hope you can come up with it somehow. Skyler's does prosecute people who leave without paying. It's called theft of service."

"Theft of service!" Natalie looked behind her. Paul impatiently tapped his foot on the floor, waiting for payment. Natalie turned back around and pleaded with Kevin. "Look, Kevin, please come back and pay this bill. Hate me if you want to, but don't leave me in this position. You're the one who ordered three entrees, not me."

"Sorry, Natalie, or whatever your name is, but I'm afraid I can't help you out."

"You idiot!" she screamed. "How can you justify doing this to me?"

"Let's see… What was that you said to me when I asked you how you could justify your deceptiveness these last few months? Oh that's right, you said, 'I don't have to,'" Kevin retorted sarcastically and hung up.

Kevin's demeanor toward her was undoubtedly dramatically different than it had been just twenty-four hours ago. Last night he had expressed his willingness to explore the possibilities of their relationship now that he and Wendy were getting a divorce. Having pursued this man—and his money—for months, the words were soothing to Natalie's ears. Somehow, between yesterday and today, Kevin had learned that Natalie had befriended him using her middle name purposely to conceal from him that she and Wendy had been friends since high school.

Natalie and Wendy had lost contact when she'd moved to New York, and it was during this time that Wendy and Kevin had married. They were already separated by the time Natalie came back to Ohio, so, when the opportunity to get to know Kevin appeared, Natalie took it. Sure, there were other well-to-do men in Columbus, but it made no sense to let Kevin get away…especially since Wendy had told her so much about him.

Being the "middle man" provided Natalie with the perfect opportunity to manipulate the couple's situation. She had urged Wendy to "move on" while advising Kevin to file for divorce. Natalie knew that she would have to admit her dishonesty to Kevin eventually. She'd planned to do so well after the divorce was final, hoping by then Kevin would be willing to overlook her transgression. However, tonight he'd angrily confronted her and Natalie now realized that this whole evening had been a set-up. "Ugh!" she grunted.

"Ma'am, is there a problem?" Paul asked, appearing unsympathetic to her plight.

"No, there's no problem.... I—"

"I take it your gentleman friend is not coming back."

"No, but that's okay," she said, nervously biting her bottom lip while trying to think of a solution. Her first impulse was to try and charm her way out of this unfortunate situation. Maybe she and Paul could work out a deal. On second thought, Paul looked too serious to be overcome by any type of female persuasion. Besides, the gentle sway in his walk suggested that Kevin was more likely his type than she was.

"Ma'am, I'm afraid that if you don't pay, I'm going to have to get the manager."

"Hold your horses, will you!" She frantically punched numbers on her cell phone. She really didn't want to call Richard, but there was no other choice. It's not like her mother could get up from the hospital bed to come and help her out. Natalie was totally out of options—she had to call him.

"Great!" Natalie uttered as the voice mail kicked in and she prepared to leave a message. "It's Natalie. Um...I need a favor. I'm downtown at Skyler's. My date left me with the bill and no money. Can you please help me out?" she pleaded.

"I'll be right back with the manager," Paul insisted.

"No! Wait—" Natalie tried to object, but her words trailed behind Paul as he stormed off. How in the world would she get out of this mess? She desperately glanced around the private dining room looking for a way out. There was no way to escape except by going through the main restaurant. If she hurried, maybe she could leave before Paul returned with the manager.

With her heart pounding at three times its normal rate, Natalie took off her two-inch heels before grabbing her purse and her suede, knee-length coat, then sprinted toward the door. The adrenaline rush was almost more than she could handle, except it was quickly subdued; she opened the door to be met by Paul and a tall, stocky, dark-haired man who looked more like a bouncer than a manager.

"Going somewhere?" the manager smirked.

Chapter 2

Short and Simple

Natalie tried calling Richard again after she'd been taken to jail—still no answer. She left another message, stressing the urgency of the matter. Under Ohio law, because the restaurant bill was over five hundred dollars, she was arrested on a fifth-degree felony theft charge.

Now, trapped inside a holding cell, her sexy black dress replaced with a plain light-brown shirt and green pants—compliments of the Franklin County Corrections Center—Natalie quickly glanced around. With the exception of one heavyset woman who was propped up in the corner of the cell sleeping, the other women looked up briefly when Natalie entered. No one said anything to her, but soon returned to their conversations. Frightened by her circumstances, Natalie stood frozen. She wasn't a criminal and didn't like being treated like one. She'd watched movies about women in jail before. What if she got jumped, or even worse, raped!

Silently she pleaded with God to get her out of this situation. But, having nothing to offer Him in exchange, she felt her prayers were in vain. She would vow never to date another married man again, but she wasn't sure she'd be able to keep that promise…especially if the right one came along. She didn't mind dating married men who weren't going to remain married, but Natalie demanded too much attention to be someone's permanent mistress. The one thing she knew for sure was that she'd never date Kevin again. That was definitely a commitment she'd be sure to keep.

"You'll probably be here for a while," called out a Caucasian woman with a boyishly short hairstyle. She looked around Natalie's age, maybe a few years younger. "You might as well make yourself at home, sweetie."

The woman had to be a repeat offender in order to say something so stupid. How could Natalie possibly make herself at home in this place? And what was up with the pet name? *Sweetie?* Natalie didn't like that inference. Was the lady coming on to her? Just to make it perfectly clear that she wasn't interested in having *any* type of relationship, Natalie slowly walked over and took a seat on the opposite side of the cell from where the Caucasian woman was sitting.

"This is your first time, ain't it?" another lady asked. She was Black, her hair pulled back into a ponytail.

Natalie nodded yes. The woman reeked of alcohol, but didn't show any obvious signs of being drunk. Her speech wasn't slurred nor did her eyes appear to be glassy. She just stunk.

"Don't get too paranoid. You're in the county jail, not the female penitentiary. Nothin's gonna happen to you in here," she assured. "What's your name?"

Natalie answered, praying her voice wasn't shaking. She didn't want people to know how scared she was.

"Well, Miss Natalie, I'm Jacqueline, but my friends call me Dee. It's short for Denise, my middle name. Whatcha in for?"

"Theft," Natalie reluctantly answered, sickened by the stench of the woman's breath. It was just as assaulting as her body odor. Somebody really needed to pour some mouth-wash down her throat.

"When you go to your arraignment hearing, make sure you plead not guilty," she advised. "See, if you plead guilty, the case will automatically be over. Whatcha wanna do is make them prove your case to a jury." She pointed at Natalie as if she was scolding her. "All you need is reasonable doubt to be scot-free, baby!"

When the woman called her "baby," Natalie's heart raced. Maybe Jacqueline was coming on to her now. "I...um, this seat isn't too comfortable. I'm gonna try and sit somewhere else." She sprang up and moved to a different part of the cell. This time she chose to sit between the heavyset woman sleeping in the corner and an unattractive, dangerously skinny Black woman leaning sideways against the cement wall, her back toward Natalie. At least that's how the thin woman was positioned when Natalie first sat down. Within seconds, she turned and faced Natalie.

"Whatcha in for?" she asked, her front teeth missing.

Natalie groaned, closed her eyes, and laid her head back against the wall. It was going to be a long night.

"Coleman..." the guard called out about an hour after Natalie had come back from her arraignment hearing the next morning. Bond had been set and paid, and a pre-trial hearing was scheduled for six weeks from now. "You're free to go," the guard announced.

Richard must have finally gotten her message. If only she could've reached him at the restaurant. Spending the night in this place was horrible, and unfortunately there was no VIP section. As if being humiliated at the restaurant hadn't been enough, she'd been locked up with women who, in her opinion, were inferior to her. They had *real* issues like drugs and prostitution, unlike Natalie, who merely didn't have enough money to pay for dinner.

I could just kill Kevin, Natalie thought to herself as she changed out of the jail uniform back into her black dress. Unhumbled by the experience, Natalie had a speech decorated with profanity ready to deliver to Kevin later. In all of her life, she had never been rejected to such an extent by any man. She honestly didn't know what upset her more: the fact that she'd spent the night in jail or that she'd been dumped in such a public and mortifying manner.

"You need to sign here, indicating that you are receiving all of your belongings." A lady instructed, shoving a paper and Natalie's personal things toward her.

She leafed through her confiscated items. Everything seemed to be intact. She scribbled her signature on the paper. Moments later she anxiously waited as the woman in the control room buzzed her out.

"Nat…" Richard smiled and greeted her with open arms. He had on a dark-gray pinstriped suit and a black leather trench coat. His attire seemed to complement his dark-brown complexion. His leather beret covered up his slightly graying hair. Richard and Natalie's mother had been dating on and off for several years. For a middle-aged district attorney, he didn't look too shabby, although he could stand to lose a few inches around his waist.

"Hello, Richard," she said dryly, ignoring the invitation for a hug.

"Do you need to get your car from the restaurant?"

"No, I just need you to take me home." She whizzed past him.

The February air was cold and crisp. Natalie could see the sun peeking through the clouds, but it wasn't warm enough to diminish the chill she felt in such a revealing outfit. Last night, it had seemed the perfect thing to wear. It didn't matter that it was cold then. Her temperature had been rising in anticipation of what she'd thought she would be doing with Kevin after dinner.

Richard deactivated the alarm on his silver Lexus with his key chain and opened the door so Natalie could get in. The lingering smell of cigarettes choked her and she began coughing. He was a classic chain smoker, yet her mother was the one in the hospital with cancer—talk about irony! Her mother developing cancer seemed not to have affected Richard at all in terms of swaying him to quit smoking, at least not that Natalie had been aware of. The open pack lying in his cup holder combined with the suffocating smell of his car made it obvious that, if Richard had made any type of vow to stop smoking, his pledge had expired.

Natalie had lost track of the number of times that Richard had quit over the years. During Natalie's last year of college, Richard's father had unexpectedly died of a heart attack. Like Richard, his father had been a chain smoker, but was otherwise considered healthy. Natalie recalled how, during the months immediately following his father's death, Richard had gotten on a serious health-conscious kick. He'd given up cigarettes, stopped eating red meat and pork, and had bought himself and Natalie's mother memberships to one of the local gyms. His father's death seemed to have scared him straight; that is until Richard started prosecuting several high-profile cases. Soon, the gym memberships went unused, pork and red meat became regular items in his diet, and cigarettes were once again his friends. Since then, Natalie had witnessed or heard from her mother about other attempts

Richard had made to—once and for all—"kick the habit," but apparently he had never been successful.

Shortly after leaving the jail parking lot, Richard was headed east on I-70, going toward Reynoldsburg, the Columbus suburb where Natalie and her mother lived. He reached into the cup holder and pulled out one of his cigarettes, quickly lighting it up.

"I know this is your car, but can you please refrain from smoking? I happen to like ingesting clean air into my lungs and it's too cold to ride with the windows down."

Richard took one good puff before extinguishing his cigarette in the ashtray and leaving it to rest for later. "What's up with the attitude?" he asked.

"If you had to spend the night in jail, you would have an attitude also."

"Yeah, well I'm not the one who put you there, so you can quit acting like it."

"Sorry…I'm just anxious to get home, take a shower and get some sleep."

"So, do you want to tell me what happened last night?"

This was why she didn't want to call him in the first place. She knew he would press her for information because he interrogated people for a living. "I told you in the messages I left. I didn't have enough money to pay for the bill at Skyler's," Natalie answered in a less-than-tolerant tone.

Richard seemed to ignore her cynicism. "*Why* did your date leave you at the restaurant?"

Knowing he would not stop grilling her, Natalie decided to give him a very abridged version of what had happened. "To make a long story short, there were some complicated issues with his wife." There, that was short and simple. No need to go into detail about things.

"Did you know he was married beforehand?"

"Yes."

"Natalie!" he exclaimed. "How could you purposely date a married man? Don't you realize the sacredness of a marital relationship?"

She quickly regretted telling him anything. His ex-wife had committed adultery and Richard was very judgmental of people who engaged in extramarital affairs. God only knew what he'd say to Natalie if he knew the whole story and how she had added to the complications of Kevin and Wendy's marriage. "Look Richard, think whatever you want. I'm really too tired to care right now. He and his wife were separated when we first met. The fact is, I am no longer involved in that relationship, and don't ever intend to be again. I've never told my mother about him, and I hope you won't either."

Richard shook his head in disbelief. "I am really disappointed in you, but I won't tell Sharon. In light of her health problems, she doesn't need anything else to worry about. You need to be careful, though. It's never a good idea to become involved with a married man. If he's willing to violate his marriage vows, then he certainly wouldn't be true to you. I never imagined you as the type who would—"

"Yeah, well there's a lot about me that you don't know..."

"Apparently..." Richard said sarcastically, then softened his tone. "Look, sweetheart, I'm sorry if I sound judgmental. Natalie, you are such a beautiful and bright young lady. I don't want to see you sell yourself short. I'm just telling you what I would tell my own daughter."

Blah, blah, blah... "I am not your daughter, and you are not my father. Let's remember that, okay?" Before he could have a chance to fully digest her words and respond, Natalie reached down and turned the radio up loud enough that his voice would be drowned out if he dared to speak again. She laid her head back on the headrest and listened to the smooth sounds of jazz infiltrate the air.

Maybe you were a little harsh, she scolded herself. She had to admit, Richard had been there for both her and her mother over the years. He had only been divorced a few years when he and her mother had first met. Richard's marriage was dissolved after he'd found out that his wife was having a long-time affair. The daughter that he'd supported and raised was, in fact, someone else's. Amazingly, he seemed to have overcome his trust issues because several years ago, he'd proposed to Natalie's mother who had turned him down—hence the off-and-on relationship. Still, Richard was always there whenever Natalie or her mother needed him most. Natalie knew Richard meant well with the advice he had given her, but she felt she was no longer in need of a father figure. At the tender age of five, she'd seen fate step in and take her daddy away.

Natalie vividly remembered sitting on the living-room sofa with her mother watching television as the two of them waited for her father to come home from work. Back then, Natalie and her parents lived in Jackson, Mississippi. Her father worked full-time at the railroad while her mother, who had been disowned by her parents for marrying a Black man, worked part-time as a waitress. Sharon had just finished preparing dinner, which was being kept warm in the oven because they were waiting for Natalie's father to come home. Whenever James Coleman walked through the door, Natalie would always run and jump into his arms. He would swing her around and smother her with kisses before changing out of his work clothes, and then the three of them would sit at the table and share their meal, just like the families on TV did at that time.

Natalie remembered how, after several hours, her mother began making phone calls to relatives, but apparently no one had seen or heard from him. Natalie could still hear the horrifying scream her mother had belted out when a police officer showed up at the door. Peering in and seeing Natalie, he took Sharon aside and whispered something to her. Not knowing what the man said, Natalie began crying just because her mother was crying and it scared her. Soon, their home was swarming with teary-eyed relatives.

Still scared and confused, Natalie asked her mother "When is Daddy coming home?" No matter what was happening, she knew her father's presence would make her feel safe. It always did—in the middle of the night during thunderstorms or when she heard noises under her bed, there was something about being in her father's arms that gave Natalie a sense of security. To Natalie's dismay, her mother tearfully replied, "I'm sorry, sweetie, Daddy's not coming home." It was then that Natalie had learned the cause of all the sad faces around her—her father had been killed in an automobile accident. That had been over twenty-five years ago, but if Natalie pondered the memory of that night too long, it seemed like it had just happened yesterday.

After her father was killed, things seemed to change drastically. She and her mother moved in with her paternal grandparents for a while. By the time Natalie was nine, the well-to-do Jesse Baxendale had charmed his way into her mother's life. Nearly five years later, that marriage was dissolved and she and her mother fled from Jackson and began growing roots in Ohio.

The circumstances under which they'd left were not the greatest, and Natalie sometimes wondered how her life would have been had they stayed. Her father's death wasn't the only hole that had been left in her heart. One issue continued to remain a mystery. People wondered why, at age thirty, Natalie seemed so self-centered and callous. True, her heart had become hardened, but her life experiences had trained her to be that way. It wasn't that she didn't want to care about other people; she was just too afraid to let herself do so.

Natalie must've dozed off during the ride because when she opened her eyes, Richard was pulling into the driveway behind her red Camry, with its personalized Q T PIE license plate. Richard turned the radio down and pushed the gear to Park. "I thought you'd like to know that I talked to the owner of Skyler's. He's agreed to drop the charges if you pay the bill, but you are no longer welcome there. You need to call him to work out the restitution arrangements. His name is José Romano."

"Yeah, well I can't say that I'm anxious to return there, so that's fine with me," Natalie said as she mustered up the energy to open the car door.

Richard grabbed her by the arm. "It wouldn't hurt for you to show a little gratitude and say thank you. I'm scheduled to be in court in less than an hour. I dropped everything to come and bail you out of jail, you know."

Natalie jerked away. "My bad…thanks."

Chapter 3

A Godsend

As Richard peeled out of the driveway, Natalie walked up to the house, stepping over the newspaper lying at the bottom of the short flight of stairs to the front porch. She'd get it later. *Home at last!* she thought when she walked into the spacious living room. After a night in the slammer, she had a new appreciation for the beige sectional, oak coffee and end tables, and the matching entertainment center holding a twenty-seven-inch TV along the back wall. Natalie's mother had single-handedly chosen the decor of the house. Natalie's decorating style was more contemporary. Other than her bedroom set, she had sold all of her furniture before moving back from New York, figuring there wouldn't be enough room in her mother's house to store it.

Usually at this time of the morning, Natalie was at the hospital by her mother's bedside. Sharon's prognosis, even after a double mastectomy and several other treatment combinations, didn't look very good. The illness weighed heavily on Natalie, taking a toll on her in many ways. Because her involuntary sleepover had thrown a curve in her normal routine, Natalie planned to get a few hours of sleep before going to the hospital later that afternoon.

She longed for a hot shower to wash away the grubby feeling she had from still having on last night's clothes. Plus she was sure that the smoke smell from Richard's car had clung to her hair, but both the shower and hair wash would have to wait. She stumbled down the hall and turned into her white-wallpapered, light-gray-carpeted bedroom, toppled on her queen-size bed, and immediately fell asleep.

"Natalie, please forgive me for the way I acted last night." Kevin had showed up at the door unexpectedly with a box of red long-stemmed roses. He looked as though he'd had a restless night as well, and was still dressed in the same suit that he'd worn to Skyler's yesterday evening, except it was now dirty and wrinkled. Though he looked pathetic, Natalie was too angry to feel sorry for him.

"Do you realize the position you left me in last night?" She stood in the doorway with her arms tightly folded while piercing him with her eyes.

"I know...I'm sorry. I just needed time to process everything," he explained.

"So now what?"

"Now...I'm hoping you'll forgive me so we can start our relationship over...from scratch."

"What about Wendy?"

"What about her? I don't care about Wendy. I cancelled all of my appointments today just so I could come over here and tell you that I love you. I don't want to spend another day of my life without you."

Natalie grinned slightly, knowing she now had Kevin right where she wanted him. He looked like a lovesick puppy and she was once again in control of how their relationship would play out. "You know, Kevin," she began, speaking softly, finally accepting the roses from him. "I appreciate you coming over here and all, but I'm afraid it's too late. You see, I'm no longer interested in you after the way you treated me last night. Your behavior was totally unacceptable."

"No, please don't say that." Kevin shook his head in despair. "I'm sorry. I'll do anything to make it up to you… anything!"

"Oh you fool! The only thing you can do for me is go somewhere and die. It's over, Kevin!" She slammed the door in his face, feeling justified.

"No, I love you, Natalie!" Kevin pounded from the other side. "Please don't say it's over. I love you!"

Natalie leaned her back against the door, and began to pluck petals from the roses one by one. "He loves me, he loves me not. He loves me, he loves me not," she continually repeated, laughing wickedly.

"Natalie, open up!" The frantic combination of door-pounding and bell-ringing snatched Natalie from a deep sleep. Though her dream still clung to her, she knew it wasn't Kevin at the door and rose like a zombie to answer the plea.

"Sylvia?" She was startled to see her mother's best friend. "I thought you were at some conference or something in Cleveland."

"I was…I um…"

Sylvia was also a Mississippi native. She and Natalie's mother had met in Jackson during their sophomore year of college and had become friends, despite the severe racial tensions in the south at that time. Sylvia had grown up with Natalie's father and his siblings, and so took credit for being the matchmaker between Natalie's parents. Unfortunately, Natalie's mother had never finished college because her parents had ceased funding her when she began socializing with the "Negroes," but Sylvia did earn her degree and was now the communications department chair at a local college. It was very uncharacteristic of her to be at a loss for words, so seeing Sylvia at the door struggling to speak alarmed Natalie. "What's wrong?" she prodded apprehensively.

"Um…" Sylvia's voice was low and shaky. Her eyes were watery and she bore a gut-wrenching expression. "The hospital called me…. They couldn't get hold of you or Richard…. Sharon—"

"No, please don't say it…." Natalie trembled with fear. "Don't tell me she's dead. *Please* don't—" The thick wall of protection she'd built around her feelings crumbled, and her vulnerability was exposed as tears flooded from her eyes. She found herself gasping for air and collapsed onto Sylvia's petite frame.

The days leading up to her mother's memorial service were extremely difficult. Tears raced down Natalie's cheeks every time she relived the moment she had received that dreaded message. She'd known death was a possibility, but she'd had no idea it would come so quickly. She'd thought her consultations with the doctor had mentally prepared her for the worst, but dealing with the reality of death was way different than talking about it. She couldn't stop the loneliness that burned in her chest, and she was tortured by the guilt of knowing she had missed her final opportunity to say good-bye.

When Natalie glanced at the clock it was a quarter to ten. Sylvia was due at the house any minute now. She quickly wiped her tears and managed to get her black knee-length suit on seconds before the doorbell rang. "Hey," she answered, trying to sound as though she was okay.

Sylvia, also dressed in black, wiped away the tear from the

corner of Natalie's eye before hugging her. "It's going to be all right," she whispered, crushing the brim of her hat against Natalie.

"Thanks for coming to get me."

"No need to thank me. I loved your mother like a sister. There's no way I'd let you go through this by yourself."

Natalie forced a smile. Sylvia was definitely a godsend during life-changing events. When Natalie and her mother had run away from the tragedy in Mississippi all those years ago, it was Sylvia's place that had provided a place of refuge for them. Though she was a newlywed at the time, Sylvia had selflessly opened her heart and home to them for the first three months of their transition.

Sylvia's marriage ultimately dissolved, for whatever reason, but the bond of friendship between her and Natalie's mother had endured, even through death. Sylvia had stood by Natalie's side, assisting her with all aspects of her mother's memorial arrangements. Besides a few of her former co-workers, a handful of friends, Richard and maybe a few hospital staff who had been involved with her mother's care, they didn't expect many people to attend the service; Sharon's social circle was rather small. "I'm almost ready. I just need to pin my hair up real quick."

"Okay, honey, take your time. We still have an hour before the service starts." Sylvia made herself comfortable in the living room while Natalie scooted down the hall.

While staring into the oval mirror fixing her hair, Natalie's reddened eyes asked why life had been so cruel. She'd been at the hospital at her mother's bedside faithfully morning after morning, but the one morning she didn't make it had to be the morning Sharon died. No one knew how hard it had been for Natalie to watch helplessly each day as the cancer took over her mother's body. Was it wrong for her to have a life outside of the hospital? She'd stopped pursuing her modeling career in New York just to come back and take care of her mother. Didn't that count for anything? Couldn't death have waited just a little while longer…at least until she made it to the hospital that day? Natalie now wished that she had gone, but she had made the mistake of taking time for granted, and would consequently pay for the rest of her life. Despite everything else she had done for her mother, the guilt of not being there that day gnawed away at her.

Natalie was still fixing her hair when the phone rang.

"You want me to get it?" Sylvia's voice echoed through the hall.

Though there was a phone within her reach, Natalie hollered back, "Yes, please!" being just a few hairpins away from a near-perfect French roll. If she let go now, she'd most likely have to start over.

A few moments later, Sylvia stood at the bedroom door with another house phone in hand. "It's Ida Mae."

"Oh, okay, just a sec."

"Give her a minute, she's fixing her hair," Sylvia said into the phone. "Yeah, service starts at eleven. Crystal said that she and Earl sent flowers to the funeral home." Natalie heard her say as she made her way back up the hall.

Crystal was Sylvia's younger sister and also Natalie's aunt because of her marriage to Natalie's uncle, Earl. Sylvia, still very close to several members of the Coleman family, was the one who had called down to Mississippi to inform Natalie's grandmother of Sharon's death. Natalie would have gotten around to it…eventually. She really hadn't had much contact with her father's family since she'd moved from there. In light of everything that had happened, it was easier to put the past behind her by not maintaining close connections with anyone from it.

Natalie finished her hair and grabbed the phone. "Hello."

"I'll talk to you later, Ida Mae," Sylvia said, hanging up.

"Hi, baby, how you feelin' this mornin'?" asked Natalie's seventy-two-year-old grandmother.

"I'm okay…Thanks for the card you sent. It came in the mail yesterday. I just didn't get a chance to call you."

"You're welcome. I didn't necessarily expect you to call. I just wanted you to know I was thinkin' about you."

Her words warmed Natalie's heart. She hadn't seen her grandmother or the rest of her family in a very long time— nearly eighteen years, to be exact. It wasn't as if Natalie didn't miss her grandmother. On the contrary, in the early years, she had missed her very much. There were numerous occasions when Natalie had asked her mother when they were going back to visit and Sharon would always reply, "Maybe one day." That day never came. By the time Natalie was an adult and able to make the choice to return to Mississippi on her own, the lack of consistent communication with her paternal relatives and her resolve to leave the past behind had dulled the nostalgia she had once felt.

"I won't hold you, I know you're tryin' to get ready," her grandmother continued. "If it's okay, I wanna say a quick prayer with you."

Big Mama had always been a God-of-the Bible believing-and-loving woman, so it came as no surprise to Natalie that her grandmother would be the one to offer spiritual support. "Sure, I think a prayer would be nice," she said with a slight smile.

"Father God, I thank You for this opportunity to come before You. I ask that You comfort Natalie durin' this time of loss. Will You fill the void left by Sharon's death? Lord, show her Your loving kindness, even in the midst of pain. Give Natalie strength in the days ahead. Watch over and protect her, Dear Lord. May Your presence be at the memorial service. May You touch the heart of anyone there who does not know You. All this I ask in the name of Jesus, Amen."

* * *

"Are you going to be all right?" Richard knelt down and asked after the funeral service.

Natalie dabbed her eyes with the already tear-soaked tissue and nodded. She appreciated his concern and felt bad about how discourteous she'd been to him after he'd rescued her from jail. Richard was the only man that Natalie had known her mother to become involved with since her divorce from Jesse. They'd been together since Natalie was in college, and she'd had no qualms about listing his name in the obituary, believing that her mother would have wanted it that way. Though her mother had turned down Richard's marriage proposal, Natalie knew the rejection had less to do with Richard's character and more to do with the problems that had plagued Sharon's second marriage, which had ended sourly. If her mother had accepted the proposal, Natalie was certain that Richard would have made a good stepfather. His kind nature was proven by the genuine love and care he displayed toward Natalie during her time of need. When he'd learned of her mother's death, it was as though Natalie's rude behavior earlier that day hadn't happened. His first reaction was to hold her tight, allowing her to cry in his arms, just as Sylvia had done.

"Make sure you call me if you need anything, okay?" he said to her.

"Thanks, Richard…I really mean it."

He smiled, "I know you do, sweetheart." He stood up, kissed Natalie's forehead, and then turned to Sylvia who stood nearby. "You be sure to call me, too, if you need anything."

Chapter 4

New York State of Mind

"Hi, Ms. Coleman, this is Karen with Dennison Financial Solutions. We received your application online for a financial analyst and would like to set up an interview with you if you're still interested in the position."

"Yes, of course I am!"

"Could you come in next Tuesday at two o'clock?"

"Yes, that's fine."

"Great! I'll mark you down. Do you need directions to our office?"

"You're in Westerville, right?" Natalie referred to a northeastern suburb of Columbus.

"Yes, that's correct. Off I-270 and Cleveland."

"I know exactly where you are."

"Okay. Your interview will be with Alex Jennings. If something happens and you can't make it, please call ahead of time."

"I'll definitely be there," Natalie affirmed. She couldn't afford to miss this opportunity. No matter how many times she crunched the numbers in her checkbook, things weren't looking pretty. Her mother had left a little money in a small insurance policy, but nearly six weeks after her death, that money was very close to being extinct. Thankfully, the whole legal ordeal with Skyler's was finally put behind her as she had made restitution arrangements with the owner. Now she had to find some means of keeping up with her other financial responsibilities—the mortgage, utilities and general living expenses.

Natalie's specialty was men—more specifically, men with money—and she knew she could easily live comfortably for a while by doing favors for some male associates of hers. What some would call prostitution, she called survival. Thanks to former high-school teachers, college professors and other well-to-do men, Natalie had been able to get out of many financial binds. Though tempted, she was trying not to go that route because for the amount of money she needed, getting a job was the more sensible and less tiring solution.

About forty minutes later the phone rang again. "Hello?"

"Hi, Natalie."

"Hey," she said to her grandmother. Ida Mae had consistently called her weekly since her mother's death. Her efforts somewhat helped Natalie combat her feelings of isolation. She really didn't have any friends she could lean on for support. Besides one or two calls from Richard in the weeks immediately following her mother's service, Sylvia was the only other person who'd checked in on Natalie, and now even phone calls from her were winding down.

"I just called to see what you were doin'."

"Looking for a job online."

"How's it goin'?"

"So-so… I did get a call earlier, and I have an interview on Tuesday."

"Praise God!" Ida Mae shouted.

"Don't go celebrating just yet, Big Mama. It's only an interview, I don't have the job. The way my luck's been going, I'm not going to hold my breath."

"Baby, you gotta think positive. If you go to the interview with that kind of attitude, you definitely won't get the job and you might as well stay home."

"Don't get me wrong, I'm grateful for the possibility. I just don't want to get my hopes up too high." If Natalie did get this job—or any job for that matter—after getting her finances together, she planned to move. With her mother gone, she no longer had a reason to stay in Columbus and thus she found herself in a New York state of mind.

"Well, I'm gonna be prayin' that God grants you favor. In the meantime, remember that attitude determines altitude. You'll only go as far in life as your attitude will take you."

"All I'm saying is that it's out of my control."

"It's out of your control, but not God's."

"Okay…I get your point," Natalie said, hoping this little lecture wouldn't drag.

"I'm sorry…I don't mean to fuss. I'm just concerned 'bout you. I hope you know how much I love you. I've really missed you over the years." There was a brief moment of silence, which provided the perfect opportunity for Natalie to say *I've missed you, too,* but expressing her feelings was something she wasn't good at doing. "I—I wish you'd never left, but I understand Sharon wanting to start fresh someplace where the two of you didn't have to be reminded about—"

"I *don't* want to talk about that," Natalie quickly snapped. It still hurt to recall how many powerful people in the city had turned their backs on her and her mother when their situation had come to light. Though Natalie's family had stood by them back then, their support had done little to change the final outcome of things.

"I'm sorry…I didn't mean to upset you."

"I know…I didn't mean to sound harsh….I just don't want to dwell on the past. Please promise me that you will never bring that situation up again."

"I promise. But know that if you ever want to talk about it, I'm here."

"Thanks, but I've learned to live with what happened, and I'm fine now." Natalie tried her best to sound convincing. Truth was, she had never gotten over it. How could a person really get over something like that? It was the one thing that haunted her over the years.

Chapter 5

Plan B

Clothes hangers screeched across the rack as Natalie searched for something to wear to her job interview. Her grandmother had called earlier and said a rather lengthy prayer; Natalie had unwillingly participated, not having the heart to object. Butterflies fluttered in her stomach. Why was she so nervous? She studied her slender frame in the mirror, modeling a navy-blue pant suit and ultimately deciding not to wear it. Frustrated, she ripped the outfit off and threw it on the pile of clothes already on her bed that she hadn't been satisfied with for one reason or another.

She wanted to wear the perfect outfit—one that didn't look as though she was purposely trying to get her prospective boss to notice her physical attributes, but also one that might prompt him to notice them. Sure, her grandmother had prayed for grace, favor and all that other stuff, but she'd been blessed with a gorgeous look. Why not use it to her advantage? She was interviewing with someone named Alex Jennings. The one thing Natalie knew for sure about men was how to get their attention.

"Ta-dah!" She nestled into a tan jacket and a skirt which stopped just above her knees. It wasn't too short, but it did show off her slender, long legs. Most guys were suckers for long legs. With luck Mr. Jennings would be, too. The suit jacket came down low enough that it didn't look sleazy, but he could get a good look at her cleavage—if he wanted to. It wasn't as if she was planning to sleep with the man. She just wanted to use her looks to get her in the door, then she'd show Mr. Jennings that in addition to being beautiful, she also had brains. Satisfied with her apparel, she carefully applied makeup, sprayed a hint of perfume and headed out the door.

"Excuse me," a man said and brushed past Natalie as he stepped off the elevator. Following the instructions given to her by the receptionist, she headed to the second floor as the elevator groaned on its way up.

"Hi, are you Natalie?" a middle-aged woman with auburn hair was waiting to greet her.

"Yes…"

The lady extended her hand, "Nice to meet you. I'm Alexis Jennings, but please, call me Alex. I'm one of the senior managers here and the person you'll be interviewing with today."

What! A warm feeling of embarrassment came over her. "Nice to meet you, too." She forced a smile and shook Alex's hand, wishing she'd worn something else.

"Follow me, I'll take you into my office and we'll get started." Alex led Natalie to a set of secured double glass doors where she swiped her identification card. They walked through a set of cubicles. Several heads turned and smiled

Natalie's way as if to wish her "good luck." Without drawing suspicion, Natalie tried to tighten the gap of her suit jacket, but without some extra material and safety pins her efforts were useless.

"Please, have a seat," Alex instructed once they were inside her office. Besides a couple of framed degrees, and a picture on her desk of what appeared to be her family, there weren't any personal items.

Natalie sat down on the dark-blue, cloth-covered guest chair on the other side of Alex's desk, gently tugging her skirt down and making sure her knees stayed glued together. Her plan to silently seduce her way into employment was crumbling and she was a nervous wreck. Time for plan B— draw on the things her grandmother had said. Something about attitude...

"Let me tell you a little about Dennison Financial Solutions," Alex took her seat on the other side of the desk. "The company was started in 1987 and provides a range of services to other companies and individuals. We do everything from preparing budget and revenue projections for our various subsidiaries to giving financial advice. There are eleven branches throughout the U.S. The main location is in Florida and besides this office in Ohio, there are three in California, two in New York and one each in Arizona, Texas, Wisconsin and D.C."

Natalie was especially interested in the New York offices, which could offer the possibility of a transfer.

"I am one of three senior managers here—" Alex continued. "There's one of us on each floor. We each oversee a different aspect of the company. The people who work with me deal more with small businesses which gross one hundred thousand dollars or less. We'll get more into the ins and outs of Dennison later. Now, I want you to tell me about you. I've read over your résumé very thoroughly, so I already know you have a finance and business administration degree, and I'm aware of your previous work experience. I say that because usually at this part of the interview, people start repeating everything that their résumé stated. I already know you look good on paper, or else you wouldn't be here. Right now you must make yourself look good in person, too. First, list three attributes you have that make you right for a position with our company."

Alex locked her eyes on Natalie, causing her a bit of discomfort. Maybe it was just paranoia, but she felt as though there was a you-have-some-nerve-coming-to-an-interview-dressed-like-that meaning behind Alex's gaze. Natalie refused to even look down at her chest, afraid of what her own reaction would be if she saw her girls peeking out. Instead, she answered as confidently as she could under the circumstances. "I'm a multi-tasker. I enjoy working on several different projects at a time, yet I'm still able to give each one adequate attention in order to ensure accuracy. I'm flexible. Whether I'm working alone or with a team, I will make sure the job gets done. Finally, I handle pressure well. I'm sure you probably already know being a financial analyst can be stressful at times." Natalie watched as Alex nodded her head in agreement. "Be it deadlines, multiple reports, fiscal budgets or whatever—I'm not one to crack under pressure."

Alex jotted down a few notes and then asked, "Where do you see yourself at in five years?"

Living in a fancy New York penthouse, signed with a top modeling agency, and traveling all over the world, was what really came to mind. She hoped her modeling career would finally take off when she moved back to New York. Technically, Natalie was considered "old" in the modeling world, despite the fact that she was only thirty. But, she believed that her portfolio was strong enough to compensate for her age.

Even if she couldn't have longevity in modeling, it would at least open the door to other possibilities like acting. For the time being, however, Natalie knew she had to tailor her ambitions and answer Alex's question accordingly. "I see myself gaining more experience in the financial field over the next five years, thus being better equipped to serve others, and being an asset to the company I'm with."

Over the next twenty minutes or so Natalie tried her best to give satisfactory answers to each question thrown her way.

"That's all I have," Alex announced after she had finished her interrogation. "It was a pleasure interviewing you today. There are a few other candidates I'm considering as well. I'll contact you by Thursday if I decide in your favor."

"Okay…" Natalie tried to sound hopeful, but Alex's words weren't too assuring.

By Friday afternoon Natalie was back at square one looking through job listings on Monster.com. When she told her grandmother that she hadn't received a call yesterday, Big Mama had gotten all spiritual on her again, reminding her that "God was in control." Whatever!

"Hello?" she answered the phone reluctantly, assuming it was Big Mama calling back to give another sermon.

"Hi, is this Natalie?" a woman asked.

"Yes…"

"This is Alex Jennings from Dennison Financial Solutions." She perked up. "Hi, how are you?"

"Good. I apologize for not calling you by yesterday as I'd promised. It took a little longer for me to come to a decision than I thought it would."

Natalie wondered if her apparel had had anything to do with the delay.

"However, if you're still interested in working for us, I'd like to offer you the position."

"Yes!" Natalie exclaimed.

"Good...I know it's late notice, but will it be a problem for you to start on Monday?"

"No, not at all."

"Great!" Alex said and quickly went over the things Natalie would need that day. "It's important that you bring proper identification to ensure your paperwork is processed in a timely manner, and that you get your first paycheck on time."

"I will."

"Do you have any questions before Monday?"

"No."

"Okay. I'll see you then at seven-thirty. Have a great weekend."

"Thanks, you, too." Natalie was excited. Is this the favor Big Mama had prayed for the morning of the interview? Natalie quickly dialed her grandmother's number.

"Guess what...I got the job!" She laughed as shouts of "Hallelujah" and "Praise God" darted from Big Mama's lips.

Chapter 6

ESP

Natalie made it to work with just minutes to spare because of excessive traffic due to a highway shut-down. Luckily, the day didn't drag on thanks to a meeting with Alex and the mountain of files she had yet to familiarize herself with. Her coworkers seemed like okay people. Everyone pretty much kept to themselves. Everyone except Aneetra Bennett.

"Hey, girl, I was looking for you around lunchtime."

Natalie cringed when she heard the voice of Aneetra behind her. She turned to face her, "Why were you looking for me?" she asked, already knowing the answer to her own question.

"To invite you out to lunch."

How many times would Natalie have to say no before this woman stopped asking! Aneetra was the only one relentless in her pursuit to get to know Natalie on a more personal level, as if she wore a sign that read, Hi, I'm Natalie and I Would Like You to Be My Friend. Besides that, Aneetra's constant tune-humming and happy-go-lucky-I-never-seem-to-have-a-bad-day attitude could be aggravating at times. Maybe she felt that they had to have some type of relationship since they were the only two Black female employees on the second floor. They seemed to be around the same age, give or take a few years. What would it take for Aneetra to realize that the whole sistah-let's-stick-together routine was not going over well? "I wouldn't have been able to go anyhow," she answered. "I packed my lunch today." That was a lie.

Aneetra pushed some folders aside and sat her approximately size-fourteen figure on the corner of Natalie's desk.

Natalie wanted to tell Aneetra to respect her personal space, but she'd only been with Dennison a few weeks. Until she was past her ninety-day probationary period and her employment was etched in stone, she wouldn't risk making any enemies. Plus, Aneetra's warm smile made it hard to be rude.

"Well, maybe we can go another time."

Maybe not…

"Are you all right?" she asked.

"Yeah, I'm fine." Natalie told yet another lie. Truthfully, she was battling depression. Today's date was May tenth, her thirty-first birthday. This was the first year that she hadn't been awakened in the wee hours of the morning by her mother singing a severely off-key rendition of "Happy Birthday." Not the most pleasant sound, to say the least, but it was one of those small gestures that Natalie now realized she had taken for granted. Tears burned her cheeks this morning as her heart begged to hear the sound of her mother's voice one more time. Instead, silence had consumed the air.

"You seem a little different today. Girl, I know it may seem like I talk a lot…"

Gee, I hadn't noticed…

"…but, I'm a good listener, too. If you ever need to talk, I'm only a few cubicles away."

"Thanks, but I'm fine," she reiterated, feeling self-conscious. Had her distress shown on her face? She'd always thought she was good at hiding her emotions, yet Aneetra sensed something wrong. Did the woman have ESP? Natalie definitely wanted to keep her distance. The last thing she needed was someone knowing more about her than she was willing to share.

"So, what do you think?"

"Huh?" Natalie had obviously missed something.

"I asked if you thought the O&M projection for the McMillan account seemed reasonable."

"Oh…well, considering that his company hasn't turned a profit in two years, I'd say it's a bit underestimated. I'd increase it by about five percent."

"That's what I thought, too, but Ron suggested I leave it be. I just wanted a second opinion. Well, I'm gonna go back to my desk and get some work done." Aneetra got up and put the papers she'd pushed aside back where Natalie had originally had them. "I know you said you were tired, but I really do sense that something else is going on with you. I won't press you to talk about it, though. But if you ever change your mind and feel like talking, just let me know. In the meantime, I'll be praying for you, okay?"

Natalie rolled her eyes after Aneetra left. That was another thing that drove her crazy—Aneetra was some kind of prayer fanatic. It was different when Big Mama offered to pray for and with her. Old folks did things like that. And, anyhow, Natalie's grandfather had been a preacher, so naturally her grandmother was accustomed to praying. Offers from Aneetra seemed awkward. In some ways she reminded Natalie of Kevin's wife, Wendy, but deeper.

Wendy had always pretty much been a Goody Two-shoes, going to church and never doing or saying anything out of the way. But when things started going bad between Wendy and Kevin, Natalie had witnessed her former friend stray further and further from her Christian upbringing. Aneetra, on the other hand, seemed to be much more grounded. Though she didn't walk around wearing an I'm-a-Christian badge, Aneetra's consistent behavior made her religious beliefs obvious. Natalie just wished that girlfriend would learn to leave her alone. If she wanted Aneetra's prayers, she knew how to ask for them.

When Natalie got home from work there was a message waiting from her grandmother. It felt good knowing that her birthday hadn't completely been forgotten. Big Mama stated that she would've called her at work or on her cell phone, but she had misplaced those numbers.

"Hey, it's Natalie," she said into her grandmother's answering machine, "I know you said you probably wouldn't be home this afternoon in your message, but I still wanted to call and thank you for the birthday wish." She quickly gave her both alternate numbers again. "If you can, give me a call later. I'll talk to you soon."

Listening to Big Mama's message was definitely a picker-upper, so Natalie saved it just in case she needed a lift later. She wondered if she would hear from Sylvia at all today. It would be nice, considering they hadn't spoken in almost a month. The other day Big Mama had said something about Sylvia dating some guy and mentioned how happy she and Sylvia's sister, Crystal, were to learn that Sylvia was finally trusting men again after going through such a horrific divorce. Natalie didn't know the particulars that had led to the divorce, since Sylvia's marriage had fallen apart when she was living in New York. She didn't even know much about Sylvia's ex-husband. Though she and her mother had lived with them for a few months upon moving to Ohio, getting to know an adult man was not one of Natalie's priorities then. From what she remembered, he seemed to be a pretty nice guy. In any event, if there was indeed a new beau in Sylvia's life after years of being alone, that would certainly explain why Natalie hadn't heard from her—she was probably making up for lost time.

Chapter 7

Morality Card

"Are you from Columbus?" Aneetra asked while chomping on a pack of candy one Friday as she and Natalie sat together in the break room.

"No, I'm originally from Mississippi."

"Really? I'm a country girl myself. I grew up in Louisiana. Most of my family still lives there. How'd you end up in Columbus?"

Natalie took a sip of her bottled water. Whenever anyone asked that question, it always made her feel uncomfortable. There was the truth, then there was the story that she told everyone. "My mom was looking for better job opportunities. Her best friend lived up here, so we moved here when I was thirteen. I've been here ever since—except for the years I lived in New York."

"Did you go to college in New York?"

"No, I went to Ohio State. I was pursuing a modeling career in New York."

"How neat! I can picture you being a model. You're very pretty."

"Thanks." Natalie was a bit surprised. Because the modeling industry was so competitive, she wasn't used to getting comments like that from other females, especially Black ones. Natalie felt that most African-American women didn't truly consider her to be one of them because she was half white. She assumed that many Black women were afraid to give her any props because they were dealing with their own insecurities. But Aneetra was different. Although she wasn't drop-dead gorgeous, she exhibited such confidence that Natalie almost found it intimidating.

"How'd you end up back in Columbus?"

"My mother was sick. I came to look after her last year."

"Is she doing better now?"

"Actually, she passed away in February. She had breast cancer," she answered, feeling that the conversation was getting way too personal.

"I'm sorry to hear that. My mother is very sick now." Aneetra's eyes dropped and she looked sad. "She's been having a lot of complications because of her diabetes."

"Is she still in Louisiana?"

"Uh-huh. She stays with my oldest sister. I'm the youngest of eight children. Do you have any siblings?"

"Nope…"

"How was it being the only child?"

Natalie shrugged. "It was okay. I guess I never really gave it much thought. It would be nice to have a brother or sister right now, though, who could help me find a Realtor. I'm trying to sell my mother's house."

"Girl, I can help you out." Aneetra reached in her purse and got out a business card. "This is a really good friend of mine named Lynn. She's a Realtor. Her office isn't too far from here. Sometimes we meet each other for lunch. She's really good."

Natalie took the card and put it in her purse. Although she wasn't eager to involve Aneetra or her friends in her personal life, Natalie was glad for the referral. It saved her from trying to find one herself.

"Lynn is a really sweet person," Aneetra stated. "You'll like her."

"Yeah, well I just hope it doesn't take forever to sell the house," Natalie thought out loud. The house was the biggest obstacle standing in her way of getting to New York. Luckily for her, her mother had entrusted the house to her in a deed, so it didn't have to go through probate.

"It'll all be in God's timing. Sometimes He moves fast, sometimes He moves slow. It depends on what He has planned. However, I do know for a fact that Lynn will work very hard to sell your house, so you don't have to worry about her level of commitment. She's great!"

"I'm sure she is. Thanks for helping me out. I'm going to give her a call as soon as I get back to my desk."

"Hey, before I forget—do you have plans for Memorial Day?"

"Not really. I'll probably go up to Easton or somewhere else shopping."

"Would you like to come over to my house? My husband's family is coming down from Cleveland and we're having a big cookout. You're more than welcome to join us."

No, thank you! "I don't—"

"Oh c'mon. It'll be fun. It'll make up for all those lunch invitations you've declined," Aneetra teased.

Natalie couldn't help but chuckle. "Thanks, but I don't want to intrude on your family time."

"Girl, please, you won't be intruding at all. The more the merrier." She reached back down into her purse, pulling out another business card then writing on the back. "This is my address and phone number. I live about ten minutes from here. If you change your mind, give me a call. I'd love to have you over."

Natalie slipped the card in her own purse along with Lynn's card just to be polite. She'd throw it away later.

"Something tells me you're not gonna call," Aneetra said, giving Natalie a sly grin.

There goes that sixth sense thing again.

The sun shone so brightly on Monday—Memorial Day— that Natalie was eager to get out and enjoy the nice weather. She was determined to do something fun and relaxing today since she had spent the entire weekend getting things together around the house, preparing for her meeting with Aneetra's Realtor friend later in the week. Her heart twinged when she looked out the window and saw several of her neighbors gearing up for their Memorial Day celebrations. If her mother were alive, she too, would've been outside setting up for today. *At least she's no longer suffering physically...* that fact did provide some comfort.

Natalie briefly entertained the idea of taking Aneetra up on her invitation, but quickly changed her mind. She didn't want Aneetra to assume they were more than just coworkers because they hung out together outside of work. Natalie definitely had trust issues, which stemmed from her childhood, and living in New York for a number of years, competing with other women for limited modeling positions, did not help at all. She had quickly learned that in the world of modeling it was every woman for herself. Though nothing about Aneetra seemed sadistic or petty like most of the models Natalie dealt with, she was still content with the status quo of their affiliation. Natalie got dressed in a pair of olive-green capri pants, pulled on a matching tank top and slipped on her black, low-heel, sandal-like pumps and, instead of to Aneetra's house, she headed to Easton Town Center.

The large shopping complex was packed. Instead of trying to find parking in the store's lot or on the street, she parked on the second level of the west garage. Today was the first time Natalie had gone shopping in months. She'd used her initial paychecks from Dennison to catch up on all the bills that had fallen behind. Now that everything was caught up, Natalie wanted to treat herself to a shopping spree. She promised herself that she wouldn't spend too much money, though, so as not to deviate from her overall plan of saving up and moving back to New York.

Natalie felt as though things were finally coming together. Slowly but surely, she was picking up the pieces and moving on with life after her mother's death. As she strolled toward Nordstrom, her ponytail bounced gently from side to side. Last spring she hadn't even been able to get her hair into a ponytail; by mid-February, when Kevin had left her at the restaurant, it had grown out to her shoulders, and now it extended several inches beyond. Natalie looked down at her cell phone when it rang. Just as she'd expected, it was her grandmother. "Hey, Big Mama," she cheered.

"I was gettin' ready to ask how you knew it was me, but I forgot you got that callin' information thing on your cell phone. Earl and 'nem got that, too. The telephone folks call here all the time tryin' to get me to sign up for that stuff."

"It's called caller ID…or better yet, technology." Natalie teased.

"Yeah, well I call it a waste of money," Big Mama kidded. "What are you doin'?"

"I'm out at the mall."

"You got anything else planned today?"

"No. A lady from work invited me to a cookout, but I'm not going. I don't feel like being around a bunch of people

I don't know. After I leave here, I'm just gonna go home and relax until it's time to go back to work tomorrow."

"I don't blame you. Sometimes it's good to spend time alone…. Listen, baby, I just called to say hi. I better get off this phone and finish gettin' ready. Tommy will be here any minute to get me."

"Don't you mean Uncle Earl?" Tommy and Earl were the only two of her four uncles who had remained in Mississippi. Like her grandfather, Earl, who was married to Sylvia's sister, was a preacher. From what Natalie remembered about Tommy, he'd never had a stable job or girlfriend, let alone a car to drive. Big Mama had definitely slipped out the wrong name.

"Naw, Tommy."

"But isn't he—"

"On drugs? Chile, he's been off that stuff for over nine years, and has been doin' real good. He's the director of a youth center here and is very active in church."

Natalie was speechless because she had firsthand knowledge of how strung-out her uncle had been. One time, when she was about ten or so, she was left alone at her grandparents' house while they went to take care of something at the church. Natalie was scared to death when one of the back windows shattered. Hearing someone coming through the forced opening, she ran and hid in the closet, peeking through the keyhole. She'd come out of hiding after seeing the identity of the intruder. "Uncle Tommy?"

"Uh…hey, niece…uh…nobody else is here, right?" He looked around nervously.

"No, Big Mama and Papa are at the church. Why'd you break the window?"

"Uh…about that…I, um, lost my key."

"But Big Mama said you don't live here anymore. She said you were sick."

"Naw, I'm not sick…I'm fine." Despite his claims, Tommy didn't look well. He smelled, his clothes were torn and dirty, and he was shaking like some type of epileptic. "I just saw Mama and Daddy at the church. They said I could borrow a few things, so don't pay me no mind. I'm gonna get the things they said I could take and be out of here."

Something didn't feel right about the situation, but Natalie stood frozen as her uncle went from room to room gathering any and every thing he could take with him. He even carried the living-room television out the door. Naturally, her grandparents were livid when they returned home, but not with her. Natalie cried and apologized after she'd realized what had happened. To hear her grandmother now talk about Tommy in such a positive manner was amazing. "I'm sorry, Big Mama. I just assumed that Tommy was still the way I remembered him to be."

"No need to apologize. You ain't said or done nothin' wrong. Anyhow, I better get off this phone so I can be ready when he gets here."

"Okay. I'm getting ready to go inside the store anyhow. I'll give you a call later this week."

"All right, baby, I'll talk to you later. I love you."

"I…I know." Why couldn't she bring herself to say "I love you" back? Natalie dusted off her disappointment and went into Nordstrom, heading straight for the MAC station to see what, if any, new cosmetics were available. Afterwards, she checked the women's department for items that caught her interest. She carried cash in her purse to prevent going over her shopping budget, but the way things were looking she could spend all of that in Nordstrom. Luckily, her shopping companions, Visa and Master Card, were tucked away in her purse. She'd sworn that she would only pull them out if necessary. The more she thought about it, the deep V-neck halter dress by Allen

Schwartz which had caught her attention was quickly turning into a necessity.

After Nordstrom, Natalie stopped at several other stores. When she had completed her shopping, she had spent several hundred dollars on her Visa and all of her cash. With slow, even strides, her shopping bags around her wrists, Natalie walked down Strand Street toward the indoor portion of the town center known as Easton Station, contemplating her action plan for repaying the newly charged credit card balance. She wasn't overly concerned. She had a steady income now and it wasn't likely that she'd find herself in the position she'd been in a few months ago. Besides, after everything she'd been through this year, she deserved to do something nice for herself.

Further ahead, Natalie thought she'd spotted Sylvia smiling and slowly walking in her direction hand-in-hand with a man. She couldn't get a good look at him because he was wearing a dark-blue sun visor and sunglasses. She wasn't even certain it was Sylvia. In the event that it was, Natalie pushed through the crowd so she could say hi and get a look at this man Sylvia has been calling down to Mississippi about. She kept her eye on the sun visor until she was standing directly in front of the couple. "Hey, Syl—" The words meshed in her throat and her cheeks flushed with heat. It was Sylvia all right. Standing next to her, holding her hand, was…*Richard!*

"Natalie—" Sylvia whispered as her smile faded. She and Richard quickly released their grip on each other.

Richard shoved his hands inside his pant pockets. "Hi…um, how's it going?"

Stunned, Natalie glanced from Sylvia to Richard and then back to Sylvia. This had to be some kind of joke. Surely this couldn't be what she thought—her mother's boyfriend holding hands with her mother's best friend? She quickly closed her eyes and reopened them only to find that the images before her had not changed. Disgusted by the sight of this newly formed couple, rage welled up inside her. "What do you two think you're doing?" she grilled.

"Nat—" Sylvia reached toward her, but she quickly jerked away, "Honey, I promise this isn't the way you were supposed to find out about us."

The word *us* swam laps through Natalie's head, making her feel nauseous.

"We were going to tell you," Richard added.

"Tell me what?" Her voice elevated, drawing the attention of several passersby. "That the two of you are betraying my mother by being here together? I take it Richard's the new boyfriend you've been telling Aunt Crystal about."

Sylvia remained calm, "Natalie, listen to me, honey. I know this is difficult for you to understand, but—"

"But nothing!" She glared at them. "My mother was your best friend for over three decades and here you are cozying up to someone who was her boyfriend for ten years. There is no 'but,' Sylvia. You're a disgusting whore!" she screamed, storming past them.

"Wait a minute!" Richard yelled and ran behind her.

"What!" Natalie turned toward him.

"I understand you're upset right now, but it's not fair for you to insult Sylvia by calling her names. She loves you, Natalie, and so do I. We didn't know how to tell you. This just sort of happened." Sylvia stood a few feet away, nodding in agreement.

"Oh really?" Natalie challenged. "Relationships don't just happen, Richard. People *make* them happen! The two of you had a choice and you could have chosen never to become involved. Or have you always been together? Maybe y'all were creeping behind my mother's back while she lay in the hospital dying."

"Please try to calm down. You're overreacting. It wasn't like that at all. Sylvia and I never planned this. We never so much as looked at each other inappropriately while Sharon and I were together. Our relationship didn't begin until after your mother died."

Natalie leaned closer to Richard and clenched her teeth. "In case you have forgotten, that was only three months ago. Neither one of you have an ounce of respect for her memory!"

"Natalie, I swear to you that I did not mean for things to evolve between Richard and me." Sylvia's watery eyes pleaded with Natalie for leniency.

"Oops! Y'all just accidentally fell in the bed butt-naked, right?"

"That part of our relationship is none of your business," Richard said sternly.

"I know you're upset, honey, but can we talk some place more private? You're sort of making a scene right now. No matter what's going through your head, Natalie, I loved Sharon. I miss her. More than wanting to be with Richard, I wish she was still here, but I can't change the way things have happened."

"You claimed to have loved my mother like a sister...I guess if Aunt Crystal dies any time soon, you'll be in bed with Uncle Earl next. It's like you couldn't wait for my mom to die so you could sleep with her boyfriend. Maybe you were just jealous that she managed to find a good Black man and you couldn't keep one."

"Oh c'mon Nat, that was harsh," Richard argued.

"Maybe...but what the two of you are doing is immoral and I hope you both burn in hell for it."

"You have some nerve playing the morality card, demeaning us like we're having some God-forbidden affair."

"Richard, just let her go," Sylvia pleaded.

He ignored her. "I'll admit that our relationship may be

a little unconventional, but it's not immoral. You have no right to judge us. As I recall, you're the one who doesn't mind dating married men!"

Ouch! Richard had hit a nerve. Natalie was sure that he was only making reference to Kevin, but she also knew within herself that Kevin was just one of many married men that she had dated. There was no doubt in her mind that she had been guilty of doing a lot worse than what she was accusing Sylvia and Richard of doing to her mother, and that made it difficult for Natalie to refute his statement. Instead, she spewed out a string of profanities and stormed away. Her exit would have been much more forceful had she not tripped over her own bags, sending her to the ground. "Leave me alone!" she ranted when both Richard and Sylvia tried to help her up. As she ran toward Easton Station, she spotted a security guard heading in the direction she'd just come from.

Chapter 8

Good Ol' Days

Natalie peeled out of the parking garage as fast as other cars and pedestrians would allow her to. She was so angry that her head began hurting. "I'm overreacting?" she sarcastically said out loud, reflecting on Richard's accusation. "You supposedly loved my mother and three months after her death, I see you holding hands with her best friend, and *I'm* overreacting?" Natalie floored the pedal as she hopped onto the freeway.

She wondered how Sylvia and Richard could betray her mother like that. Especially Sylvia—she and Natalie's mother were best friends! Sylvia had some nerve going out with Richard as though the friendship didn't mean a thing. Deep down, Natalie knew that Wendy had probably asked the same question about her, but she tried to convince herself that her involvement with Kevin was totally different than Sylvia's involvement with Richard.

Part of the reason Natalie was so angry was that if Sylvia

and Richard had been upfront with her she still would've been upset, but maybe she would've done away with the name-calling…maybe. The whole situation disgusted her. She was madder at Sylvia than Richard. Richard was a man. Like every other man, he most likely made decisions with his third leg rather than his brain. But, Sylvia? Sylvia was her mother's best friend. How could she do this!

Sure, there had been some obstacles in her mother's and Richard's relationship—Sharon's fear of marrying again being the biggest one—but other than that, they seemed to get along well. Natalie wondered if Sylvia would have dated Richard if he and her mother had actually married. She was willing to bet that if there were any signs of trouble in their marriage, Sylvia would have befriended Richard behind her mother's back. Yeah, Natalie had betrayed Wendy, but her situation with Kevin was different. She had not renewed her friendship with Wendy with the intention of backstabbing her. Things with Kevin just hap— "Ugh!" Natalie grunted and pounded her fist against the steering wheel as she sped down the freeway. Why couldn't she just be mad at Sylvia without finding similarities to her own actions? Her situation with Kevin was different. She couldn't explain why it was. It just was.

"This is just great!" she murmured, seeing flashing red and blue lights in her rearview mirror.

"Ma'am, do you know why I pulled you over?" The stocky officer asked.

"Uh-huh." She took the liberty of handing him her documents before he had a chance to ask for them.

"I clocked you going eighty-seven in a sixty-five-mile-per-hour zone. Do you mind telling me why you were going so fast?"

"What does it matter? I'm going to get a ticket anyway, right?"

"With that type of attitude, yes, you are. Seeing that it's

a holiday and I'm a fairly nice guy, initially, I was going let you off with a warning if everything panned out. But now just hang tight," the officer sneered and went back to his car.

Natalie sighed and laid her head back on the headrest. Her head hurt so badly; she just wanted to get home. She continued to sit in agony until the officer came back.

"Here's all of your stuff back. You're receiving a speeding citation today," he noted as if the pink slip he handed her wasn't proof enough. "The fine must be paid within ten days either by mail or in person. If you feel that you're receiving this citation without cause, you do have a right to contest it in court. Your court date and time are listed on the back."

"All right…"

"Enjoy the rest of your day."

"Too late for that…" Natalie whispered under her breath. Seeing the two traitors together had killed any joy left in her. She waited until the coast was clear before swerving back onto the freeway.

Although it was nearly ten o'clock in the evening, some of Natalie's neighbor's were still outside. She lay in her bed as their voices swept through the room. Her inability to fall asleep had nothing to do with the Memorial Day celebrations going on outside her window. That noise was minimal compared to the tormenting voices inside her head.

Natalie turned from side to side restlessly, trying to position herself for a good night's sleep, but her efforts were in vain. The nagging thoughts of the day's events refused to vanish from her mind. Although still very angry at Sylvia and Richard, she was also overwhelmed with guilt. Every time she thought about what Sylvia had done to her mother, she thought about what she'd done to Wendy, and it depressed her even more that her own actions had led to the chain of events that had prevented her from being at the hospital the morning her mother died.

Desperately desiring rest for her body and mind, Natalie decided to try writing down her feelings. Writing was a technique she'd used in therapy when she was younger. Unfortunately, it hadn't done much good back then because she really hadn't practiced full disclosure. She'd known that the therapist would analyze everything she wrote down and then share his findings with her mother. Regardless of the previous results, tonight Natalie was willing to give it another shot. She turned on the lamp, searched the nightstand until she found a pen and piece of paper and began writing a poem:

> If I had known that time wasn't on my side
> I would've been at the hospital the morning you died
> I wouldn't have gone out the night before
> And thus would have prevented the guilt that I have bore
> Guilt because I feel like I somehow let you down
> What if you called out to me and I was nowhere around?

Natalie's emotions swung like a pendulum as she thought about how her mother used to love barbecuing this time of the year. She used to make a special sauce that was so good Natalie would eat it in spoonfuls. But like the early ear-piercing renditions of "Happy Birthday," her mother's signature sauce was now extinct.

> What if you reached out to hold my hand?
> I wasn't there, thanks to my desire for another woman's man
> Believe it or not, it wasn't my first time
> Going after someone who, by law, could not be mine

It's shameful to admit, but I'm not a good friend
Should I add *daughter* to the list since I wasn't there
in the end?

There was only one living person whose love Natalie
could count on—her grandmother. Big Mama was really all
she had left now. Her mother was gone, she couldn't get
over Sylvia's relationship with Richard and she had no
friends. If only her father had never died...her life would
be so different. Natalie imagined that she'd be in Mississippi
right now celebrating Memorial Day with her father's side
of the family.

A faint smile crossed Natalie's face as she reminisced
about the time when she'd lived in Mississippi. Natalie had
spent a lot of time with her grandparents, and they'd spoiled
her rotten. At the time, Natalie was the only granddaughter
amongst a group of grandsons, so naturally she had gotten
a lot of attention.

On Sundays her grandparents took her to church with
them since her mother had stopped attending regularly
after her father was killed. Big Mama would often garnish
her outfits with very big hats that sometimes would come off
during service if she was overtaken by the Holy Spirit. They
were guaranteed to come off if she was asked to sing a solo.
With a strong, angelic voice that could take on the best of
the best any day, she sang as if it was only her and God in
the church.

The church building itself was probably only meant to
hold two hundred people, if that, but Natalie could swear
that at least twice that many packed their way inside each
week. During moments of silence or prayer, the whooshing
sound of members waving hand fans could be heard. Natalie
sat on the front pew with her grandmother while her grandfather sat in the pulpit. Sometimes her cousins would sit up

there with her and they would often get in trouble for talking or playing during service. Big Mama would first give them a stern look of warning, and if that didn't settle them down, she was quick to give a pinch or slap on their thighs.

After selections by the choir and a requested solo sung by Big Mama, it would be her grandfather's turn to be heard. He was a thin man, but there was a lot of power in his messages. The heat resulting from lack of air-conditioning and attendance numbers that surely tested fire-marshall-occupancy limits did nothing to affect the impact of his sermons. By the time he finished preaching, folks were screaming out and praising God like it was nobody's business.

"Those were the good ol' days," a nostalgic Natalie whispered out loud as she wiped the tear that trickled down her cheek and splattered on to the paper she had been writing on. Those days were long over. Her grandfather was dead, the cousins she grew up with had moved away, and she hadn't stepped foot in a church since moving from there. Jackson could never be the same. Her good memories of that place had been tainted by bad ones.

Chapter 9

A Big Mess

Natalie logged onto her computer at work, wishing she could go back home, take some ibuprofin and rid herself of the splitting headache she had that morning. She'd tossed and turned all through the night, unable to erase the ghastly sight of Richard and Sylvia from her head. Even more disturbing was that everything she was mad at Sylvia for, she'd done herself. Natalie's track record for going after her friends' men dated all the way back to the time when she went out with Bobby Kendall only weeks after he and her friend, Charlene, had ended their two-year relationship.

Bobby Kendall was captain of the high-school football team and very popular among students of all grade levels. His parents were pretty well off so he drove nice cars to school, had the best clothes, and their luxury home was always the spot to hang out on Friday nights after the football games. Natalie took note of the special things Bobby did for Charlene such as buy her gifts and take her out on dates. Though Bobby didn't have a job and Natalie knew that the money he was spending on Charlene most likely came from his parents, she found herself envying the attention that her friend got.

To this day, Natalie still wasn't sure what broke Charlene and Bobby up, but she didn't waste any time throwing her hat into the ring. Like many of the other girls in the school, she flirted with him every chance she got. One day he asked her out and she gladly accepted.

Charlene didn't appear to be as bothered by Natalie's and Bobby's short-lived relationship as some of their mutual friends were. Perhaps it was because Charlene had firsthand knowledge of how much of a jerk Bobby Kendall was. Natalie received special treatment as well, but only in the presence of others. When there were no eyes observing his actions, Bobby was a complete moron. The doors he'd opened for her, she'd have to open herself; most of the gifts presented to her had to be returned, and he would sometimes ask to be reimbursed for the dates he'd publicly paid for.

Natalie didn't understand how Charlene had put up with him for as long as she had and eventually apologized to her friend for the betrayal. Truthfully, Natalie was probably more remorseful about her misjudgment of his character than she was about her actions. She did realize that it was wrong to betray Charlene, but the whole situation had happened in high school and was totally unrelated to her seeing Sylvia and Richard together. Still, considering all the venomous words she'd spat at them yesterday, Natalie now felt more uneasy about the situation with Charlene. She spent more time than necessary pointing out to herself the differences between what Sylvia was doing to her mother and her own actions.

Physically, Natalie had been at work for about an hour, but mentally—she wasn't really there. She opened a report she had been working on, and tried to concentrate on it without much success. She heard Aneetra humming and knew the perky employee would soon be her way.

"How was your weekend?" she asked Natalie moments later.

"Good…" she tried to sound believable.

"Were you able to get everything done around the house that you wanted to?"

"For the most part. I'll definitely have it together by Thursday, though. How was the cookout?"

"Girl, we had *so* much fun! I wish you'd come. My husband's family didn't leave 'til almost eleven o'clock last night. I am too tired. I almost didn't make it in today, but then I remembered that I have to finish a report for Alex today. I just hope my coffee kicks in soon," Aneetra yawned. Natalie's phone rang. "Well, I'm gonna go back to my desk so you can get that. I'll holla at you later."

Natalie took a deep breath and answered her phone.

"I'm sorry, honey, I don't mean to bother you at work." It was Big Mama. "I just wanted to call and check on you. Last night, Crystal called here sayin' that you and Sylvia had some type of fallin' out over this new boyfriend of hers."

"News travels fast…"

"I would've called you last night, but it was close to midnight when I finally got off the phone with Crystal. I knew you were asleep by then."

"I was probably up. I didn't sleep too well," Natalie admitted.

"Crystal said Sylvia was pretty upset. She wanted Crystal to call me 'cuz she knew I'd call and check on you."

"Why didn't Sylvia just call you herself? She'd call you about anything else."

"She probably didn't feel comfortable talkin' to me about somethin' like this. I don't know, baby. I'm more concerned about you than I am her."

"Don't worry about me, Big Mama, I'm fine."

"Are you sure? You don't sound like it. From what I understand, things got pretty ugly between y'all."

"I was mad, but I'm okay now. Sylvia is grown and so is Richard. Neither one of them have to answer to me." She was definitely having a problem with honesty today. She really wished she could have them both neutered to prevent them from having sex. "Big Mama, I have a meeting in a little while, so I'm gonna have to call you back later, okay?"

"Oh, I'm sorry. I didn't mean to bother you at work."

"You're not bothering me," Natalie assured. "I'll call you later this week. I have a Realtor coming by on Thursday, so this evening and tomorrow evening I want to finish doing some things I didn't get done over the weekend."

"Okay. I pray everything goes well."

"Thanks."

"I love you, sweetie." Natalie could hear the worry in her voice.

"I know—" she took a deep sigh, "I love you, too." She wasn't sure if her grandmother had even heard it. She wasn't even sure how she'd gotten the courage to say it. To her, expression of feelings equaled vulnerability, which brought with it too many risks. Love always presented the risk of getting hurt. Natalie had seen firsthand the devastation her mother had gone through when her stepfather, Jesse, had broken her heart. Though Natalie didn't believe her grandmother would do or say anything intentionally to hurt her, old habits were hard to break. Detaching herself emotionally had become one of her survival mechanisms, but for some reason, today she had let down her guard. Maybe it was because she'd reminisced last night about how things used to be when she was younger. Natalie wished she could go back to those happy times before— *Stop it!* she scolded herself. She used a tissue to wipe her watery eyes and attempted to get back to work.

* * *

"I'll call ya later, I'm gonna head on to the church," Earl got his umbrella out of the living-room closet and yelled out to his mother who sat at the kitchen table. The temperature was in the mid-seventies, but the humidity made the air feel much hotter. The warm drops of rain did nothing to cool things off. This morning Earl had stopped by his mother's house to bring back some pans she'd forgotten yesterday at his home during the cookout. He was on his way to Faith Tabernacle—the church he now led, founded by his father some forty years ago.

Earl often came by to see his mother on the way to the church. The five-bedroom, two-story brick home he'd grown up in was rich with Coleman history. He loved hearing the story of how his parents, the late Willie James Coleman and the former Ida Mae Marshall, had married when they were seventeen. A total of six children resulted from that union. Twins—Willie, Jr., and James—were the oldest, then Earl, Charles, Antoinette and Thomas. Sadly, James had died many years ago in a car accident. With the exception of Thomas and Antoinette, Earl's other siblings no longer lived in Jackson. Willie, Jr., now lived in New York and Charles lived in Florida.

"Mama, did you hear me?" Earl called out. He paused at the small piano, waiting to hear some kind of reply. His eyes quickly browsed the collection of framed pictures of various family members that sat on top, and those that hung on the nearby wall. He chuckled to himself as he often did whenever he stood next to the piano for any length of time. His parents had owned a piano for as long as he could remember, but neither Earl, his parents, nor his siblings knew how to play one. "Mama?" Earl sat his umbrella on the piano bench and walked back to the kitchen.

"I said I'm fixin' to go over to the church," he repeated, stepping on to the laminated floor.

"Oh, okay. Tell Crystal I'll give her a call later."

"You all right?" he asked, noticing the concerned look on her round face as her elbows rested on the table, her chubby hands laced underneath her chin.

"Yeah, I'm fine."

Despite her answer, Earl knew exactly what was bothering her. He pulled one of the beige wooden chairs from under the oak table and placed his tall frame next to his mother, and patted her knee. "You're worried about Natalie, aren't you?"

"Oh, Earl," she sighed in despair, "I just cain't help it."

"Now don't go gettin' your blood pressure up. Worryin' won't change anything."

"I know, but I don't think she's handlin' this whole Sylvia thing as well as she would like me to believe."

"I'm sure Sylvia and Natalie will work things out. It's just gonna take some time."

"She tried to sound as if she was mad yesterday, and today it's no big deal, but I could hear the sadness in her voice. I'm really torn. On the one hand, I'm extremely happy for Sylvia after all she's been through. She deserves to be happy after spendin' all those years in an abusive relationship. From what Crystal said, this guy really treats her nice. On the other hand, I want to slap her. Out of all the guys in Columbus, why did she have to pick Sharon's ex? She had to know that somethin' like this would hurt Natalie." Her voice cracked as she fought back tears. "It just seems like my grandbaby has been through so much in her life. I hate to see her in any more pain."

There was silence as Earl waited to see if his mother would say anything else.

A single tear dripped from Ida Mae's right eye and splattered on the back of her hand. She unlocked her fingers and wiped her hand on her pant leg. "I really miss her," she said. "It's been way too long since we've seen her."

"Yes, much too long," Earl agreed, wondering what Natalie looked like now. It had been nearly eighteen years since he'd last seen her.

"I wish she and Sharon had never moved away. Maybe—"

"Now don't get caught up in wishing you could change the past. You and I both know that's impossible. Sharon did what she thought was best at the time."

"I know, but best for who? Her or Natalie? I don't think Natalie wanted to go."

Earl shook his head in despair, "She definitely went through a lot that summer. Then to be uprooted to another state…that had to be hard on her."

Ida Mae closed her eyes as though she was envisioning thirteen-year-old Natalie again. "I want to see her *so* bad. I would invite her down here for the Fourth of July, but I'm not sure if she'll come seein' how she ain't been in all these years."

"You can always let Natalie know that she's welcome here, but don't try and put too much pressure on her to come. That's something she'll have to do when she's ready. It'll be great to see Natalie again, but I hope you're prepared for the wrath that is sure to come from you-know-who if she were ever to come back. Does she ever ask questions about—"

Ida Mae shook her head no. "I think it's too painful for her. One time, I tried to talk to her about it. Well, not really…I wasn't gonna go into detail, I was just gettin' ready to say how I hated what had happened, but Natalie snapped. She said she didn't want to talk about it—that she'd learned to live with the past and was fine now. I didn't believe her for one moment."

Earl let out a long sigh and spoke softly, "It'll be a big mess if she does come back. I would hate to be stuck in the middle of that. The truth is bound to come out. I love my family, but I love God more. If Natalie were ever to ask me, I'd have to tell her."

"I know what you mean…but I don't think she'd ever bring it up. She was too sensitive about talkin' to have gotten over it. I promised her that I would never bring it up again, and I won't. I just want her to know how much I love her."

"Mama, I'm sure Natalie knows that we all love her… especially you. I don't want you sittin' 'round worryin' about her. Remember the time during my last semester of Bible school—Crystal had just given birth to Alayah, my tuition was due, and I had gotten laid off? I was so stressed out about how I would finish school and make ends meet all at the same time. Back then, a wise woman directed me to the book of Psalm and the words spoken by David in the thirty-seventh Psalm: 'I have been young, and now am old; but I've never seen the righteous forsaken, nor his seed begging bread,'" Earl watched the slight smile spread across his mother's face as he paraphrased the twenty-fifth verse.

"Psalm is one of my favorite books of the Bible…"

"I know," he winked at her. "I believe somewhere in that great book, David also says to 'cast thy burden upon the Lord.' That literally means to throw whatever is bothering you into God's hands, leave it there and let Him deal with it. What you need to do is remember that your job is not to worry about Natalie, it's to pray for her. Then rest assured that God hears your prayers. It's impossible to worry and pray at the same time, Mama. The two cancel each other out."

Ida Mae reached out and squeezed Earl's hand, smiling affectionately. "I thank God for you," she said. "You're just like your daddy. He always knew how to use the Word of God to get me back where I need to be. You go on down to the church now, I'll be fine."

Earl stood up and leaned over to kiss her on the cheek. "I'll come back by later. If you need anything while I'm out, give me a call."

"All right, you drive careful now." Moments later Ida Mae

heard the screen door slam. "Cast your burden upon the Lord," was the first line of Psalm 55:22. God had handled so many of her concerns in years past. Surely, He could take on this one, too.

Chapter 10

Change of Heart

After a busy day at work and a long meeting with Aneetra's Realtor friend, Natalie was quite tired. Though it was only a few minutes after seven she changed into a pair of silk pajamas and spread out on the sofa with a large bowl of butter pecan ice cream, swearing to work it off at the gym next week. The meeting with Lynn had gone well. Based on her analysis, if the house sold for its listed price, Natalie would receive a nice chunk of change at the closing. It would be enough to tide her over in New York for a few months, even if she wasn't approved for a transfer through Dennison. Finally, some good news to make up for the turbulent week she'd had.

Natalie flipped through the channels, ultimately resting on Lifetime, one of her favorites, as she polished off her second bowl of ice cream. It was about a quarter to eight when the telephone rang. Willing to bet it was her grandmother calling to check on her again, she answered and could've choked on a pecan when the sound of Sylvia's voice came through and sent adrenaline racing through her body.

"What do you want?" she snarled. First thing tomorrow morning she would invest in caller ID on the home phone.

"I hope I didn't catch you at a bad time. I really would like to talk to you about what happened the other day."

"I'm not sure what there is for us to talk about. I said everything I had to say to you on Monday." Her mind flashed back to the sight of Sylvia and Richard together, but soon became tainted by visions of herself with Kevin, and other men she'd dated who were technically "off limits." Ugh! Natalie let out a heavy sigh. "But…I'm willing to listen if there's something you would like to get off your chest," she felt moved to say. "Just please make it quick."

"I'm really sorry you found out about Richard and me the way you did. You have to know that we were not sneaking around behind your mother's back." Sylvia tearfully explained. "I swear to you that I would've never done something like that to Sharon. I loved her, Natalie."

Natalie remained silent. There was a sincerity in Sylvia's voice that she couldn't argue with.

"I have not been able to get a good night's sleep since Monday. I've been trying to figure out what the right thing to do is. Truthfully, I don't know. I mean, I do love Richard, but I also love you, Nat, and I don't want to do anything to hurt you. At the same time, I feel that I deserve to be happy, and Richard makes me happy. I swear that I never planned this…I never thought I would be able to trust any man again after all the stuff I went through with Clarence. He and I met in town at a local conference years ago. Clarence was a presenter on a panel discussion about the prohibition of school prayer. As the facilitator of that discussion, I pretty much made sure things remained cordial between all participants and that they didn't run over their time limits. Clarence was so handsome and charming. He spoke with such eloquence that I clung to his every word. He asked me out that same day and we dated for several months before flying to Vegas where we eloped."

Sylvia had never spoken about her ex-husband before with Natalie, so her willingness to share details about their marriage indicated to Natalie that she seemed to genuinely be interested in making amends. Whether Natalie truly wanted to give it, Sylvia now had her undivided attention; curiosity about what had happened with Sylvia and her ex took over.

"Things were great at first, but his true character began to emerge shortly after you and Sharon moved from our house into your own place. I soon learned that my husband had two faces. In public, you'd swear he was a godly man, especially at church. Clarence did everything from serving on the deaconate board, mentoring young boys, and teaching Sunday school classes. But, at home…at home he was the incarnate of Satan. Night after night he'd beat and rape me. To make matters even worse, I went to the pastor begging for help, only to be told that my body belonged to Clarence. He even went so far as to suggest that perhaps I wasn't making myself available enough to him, and that sometimes men must discipline their wives in order to get them back in line."

"What!"

"I know! It sounds crazy, doesn't it? It took eleven years for me to get the courage to walk away. After that experience I was done with men and church folk—because neither did me any good." Sylvia paused for a moment and Natalie swore she heard sniffling. "I only said all of that so you would understand that having feelings for Richard was never something I planned. When I finally left, I swore I would never let down my guard for another man. As a result, I've only had a few superficial relationships because I was scared to trust."

Natalie could certainly relate to the fear of trusting. That seemed to be her story also.

"With Richard, the trust was already there. I already knew him. I knew he was a good man, and we were friends. I know the circumstances are odd, Natalie, but I *do* love him, and I know he loves me. I just don't know if I can live the rest of my life being happy with him, knowing that you hate me."

"I don't hate you," Natalie admitted, hoping there was no evidence of her teary eyes in her voice. "It was just very uncomfortable to see y'all together like that. I'm so used to seeing him with—"

"Your mother...I know. Getting involved in a relationship with Richard wasn't easy because of the fact that he and Sharon had spent many years together."

"How did it happen?"

"Honestly, we're still asking ourselves that question. It seemed like we were always running into each other—at the grocery store, at the gas station, at the bookstore—wherever I would go, it seemed like Richard was there, too. Whenever we saw each other, we would always joke about one of us following the other. Then, one evening I was coming home from work and my car overheated. I pulled over on the side of the freeway. While I was waiting for triple-A to come, another car pulled up behind me and when I looked up, it was Richard."

Sylvia was beginning to sound like a schoolgirl with a crush. Though Natalie still wasn't completely comfortable with the idea, she couldn't continue protesting their relationship with a clear conscience. Sylvia sounded as if she was genuinely in love, a feeling Natalie wondered if she'd ever experience.

"That night as he waited for me while the tow truck came, I think we both realized there was something other than a friendly admiration that we felt for each other."

"I won't be upset if you continue going out with Richard," Natalie finally gave in, wondering if her mother would feel the same way.

"Seriously?"

"Yes. It's going to take some getting used to the idea, but you sound like you're happy, so who am I to stand in your way?"

"Oh, Natalie!" Sylvia bubbled with joy. "You have no idea how good it is to hear you say that. I…I know that must've taken a lot of courage to say. Please know that I'm not trying to disrespect your mother's memory in any way. I did love her, Natalie, I swear."

"I know…. Listen, I'm going to get off of the phone." Natalie was starting to feel uncomfortable about the tears she was shedding. She couldn't explain her tears any more than she could her change of heart and she wanted to end the conversation fast. "Thanks for calling, but everything is fine."

"Thanks, Natalie… You have no idea what a relief it is to hear you say. I know it may still be a little awkward, but—"

"It's okay, Sylvia. I—I'm fine…really…"

"Okay…I'll take your word for it. I meant what I said earlier. I love you, Natalie. If you ever need anything—anything at all—please don't hesitate to call me."

"Thank you," Natalie replied with sincerity. Despite all that had taken place, Natalie believed that if she ever needed to, she could take Sylvia up on her offer. History had proven that when it mattered most, Sylvia would always be there.

Chapter 11

Dark Chocolate

The following Tuesday Natalie sat at her desk, still thinking about her conversation with Sylvia five days earlier. Although she had more or less given Sylvia her blessing to date Richard, truthfully, she still had mixed feelings about the whole thing. In any event, she knew it would be pointless to discuss it any further. Again, Sylvia had wasted no time calling down to Mississippi. Big Mama had called Natalie over the weekend to verify that all was well.

"How long do you think it'll take you to finish the report for the Dillon account?" Alex walked up to Natalie and asked.

"Actually, I'm done. I was going to bring it by your office later, but I can give it to you now if you want it." She reached over into her tray of finished projects and handed Alex a manila folder.

"That's a cute shirt you have on."

"Thanks." Natalie was wearing a lilac, short-sleeved, satin blouse with a pair of light gray dress pants.

"I don't see how you can wear heels like that all day long."

Natalie looked down at her open-toe, two-inch-heel sandals. "It's something I've gotten used to over time."

"I would probably break my neck if I tried wearing shoes like that," Alex stated while leafing through the papers in the folder. "I'll go over this more thoroughly later, but from what I can tell so far, you did a great job."

"Thanks."

"No—thank you. I'm glad to have you on board."

Natalie smiled.

"Keep up the good work!" Alex commended and began walking away. "Hey, before I forget—would you, by any chance, be interested in going to King's Island this weekend? If so, let me know. I have some tickets that I'm giving away. They're only good for this weekend, though, because my husband got some promo deal through his job. We were planning to drive down to Cincinnati Friday and go on Saturday, but something has come up and we can't make it."

"Shoot!" Natalie pounded her fist on her desk.

"What's wrong?" Alex looked confused.

"Sorry, when you mentioned the word *ticket* it reminded me that I still have a speeding ticket to pay."

"For a minute there I thought you'd just really hated the idea of going to King's Island." Alex laughed.

Natalie really didn't think the comment was funny, but forced a chuckle anyhow.

"Is it too late to mail your payment in?"

"Yeah, probably. I got it on Memorial Day and I only had ten days to pay it. I'll call downtown to the courthouse during lunch and see what time the clerk's office closes. I hope I can make it after work today or before I come in tomorrow."

"Don't bother calling. I know for a fact it's open twenty-four hours." Alex grinned. "I've had to make a few visits there myself. Whether you go after work today or before work tomorrow, it's going to be a bear fighting downtown traffic during rush hour."

"Yeah, I know." Natalie sighed. "Maybe I'll wait and go later on this evening if they're always open."

"I tell you what…if you want you can leave a couple of hours early today and go down to the courthouse. It'll save you from getting home and having to go back out later, but you'll have to make up your hours sometime this week."

"Seriously?" Natalie looked at Alex, surprised by the suggestion.

"Yes, I'm serious." Alex smiled. "Technically, employees aren't eligible to flex their schedules until they've passed their probation, but exceptions can be made from time to time." She winked.

"Thank you so much!"

"No problem. Just let me know before you leave today."

"Sure thing."

"Now, about these King's Island tickets…"

"Oh, no thank you. I don't have anyone to go with."

"Okay, well if you change your mind, let me know. I have six tickets, and I'm giving them away on a first-come-first-serve basis."

Natalie left work at two o'clock and headed downtown to the courthouse. The freeway traffic was pretty clear, but there was some congestion near the courthouse. Natalie circled the area several times, hoping to find an empty parking meter on one of the nearby streets. She didn't want to pay several dollars to park in one of the parking lots when it would only take her a few minutes to run inside and pay the fine.

"Finally," Natalie mumbled to herself when she observed a car a few feet ahead of her come out. She pulled into the parking space, noticing there was still eleven minutes left on the meter. She got out of her car and deposited an extra quarter just in case there was a line.

It only took a few minutes for her to walk down Mound Street and cross over High to the courthouse. Natalie placed her car keys and purse on the conveyer belt and walked through the metal detector, thinking it was ridiculous to have to go through all of this just to pay a doggone speeding ticket. After passing the security check, she went to the glass windows to pay her fine.

"You have a nice day," the clerk said, and handed Natalie a receipt.

"Thanks, you, too."

"Hey, Natalie, wait up!" She turned around and saw Richard moving quickly toward her.

Of all the people that she could've seen… There was no need trying to run away from him. The last time she'd tried that she'd ended up flat on her face.

"What brings you to this neck of the woods?" asked Richard once he'd caught up to her.

"I came to pay a speeding ticket."

"Oh. I'm glad I ran into you. I wanted to call you… I—I spoke with Sylvia."

Richard stopped for a moment as if he was expecting Natalie to say something. She wasn't sure what type of response, if any, he was looking for. It didn't take a brain surgeon to figure out that he and Sylvia had likely spoken to each other recently.

"Thanks, Natalie," Richard added.

"For what?"

"For trying to be understanding of our relationship even if you truly don't understand it."

"You're both adults. I can't forbid you to see one another."

"That's a very mature approach to take," Richard reached out and placed his left hand on her shoulder.

Natalie fought every instinct in her body to pull away, feeling the extra sentiment was unnecessary.

"I want to apologize for the harsh things I said to you at Easton. It wasn't right."

From the soft look in Richard's eyes she could tell that Sylvia had shared with him the details of Natalie's tumultuous childhood in Mississippi and the reason why she and her mother had moved to Ohio. She was certain that her mother hadn't disclosed everything to him, despite the number of years they had been dating. Natalie wondered if Richard was apologizing because he truly felt sorry for the angry words he'd spat at her or because he felt sorry for her.

"No need to apologize, Richard. I said some pretty mean things myself. So let's just call it even."

"Well—"

"So how's Columbus's best prosecuting attorney doing?" A man walked up and butted into their conversation, speaking with a very slight, Southern accent that many people would not have noticed.

Richard dropped his hand from Natalie's shoulder and shook the guy's hand. "Hey there, what's going on?"

"The same ol', same ol'. I'm really supposed to be off today, but I came down to take care of something real quick." He looked at Natalie. "I'm sorry, did I interrupt the two of you?"

Natalie shook her head no.

"Troy, this is a friend of mine, Natalie. Natalie, this is Detective Troy Evans. He's worked with the prosecutor's office numerous times over the years."

"Nice to meet you," Troy extended his hand.

"You, too," Natalie replied. Her body was incinerated with hot flashes and she tried extremely hard not to gape at the tall, smooth, dark-chocolate, sculpted frame that stood before her in a pair of jeans and a dark gray T-shirt. Immediately she placed her hand inside his firm grip, a hormonal charge shot through her veins.

"How's Mitch?" Richard asked Troy. "I haven't seen him in a while."

"He was down here the other day. He's doing good."

"Make sure you tell him I said hi."

"I will."

Richard looked down at his watch. "I better get out of here. I have a three o'clock meeting to get to." He turned to Natalie. "Thanks again for everything. Please don't hesitate to call me if you need anything. Okay?"

"Yeah, okay," Natalie responded, barely comprehending his words. Her eyes glued to Troy's and his to her.

"Troy, I'll see you around, man."

"All right, take care."

Richard hurried away, leaving the two of them together.

"Once again, it was nice meeting you." Troy extended his hand for the second time.

"Same here."

"If you don't mind me asking, what's your last name?"

"Coleman," she replied as their hands slowly drifted apart.

"Is that *Mrs.* Coleman?" Troy raised an eyebrow.

Natalie was flattered by the obvious ploy to see whether or not she was married. She smiled, held up her left hand and waved her fingers. "Do you see any rings?"

Troy laughed. "Well, *Ms.* Coleman, were you coming or going?"

"I was going."

"Did you drive? Would you mind if I walked you to your car?"

"Yes, I did drive, and no, I wouldn't mind, *Detective* Evans." She intentionally emphasized the title to his name, flirtatiously.

"Great! You lead the way," he gestured.

It had taken Natalie only minutes to walk from the parking

meter to the courthouse when she'd first arrived, but with Troy by her side, she slowed the speed severely. "So, how do you know Richard?" he asked as they stood at the intersection of High and Mound waiting for the crosswalk signal to change.

"He was a friend of my mother's." She felt it was unnecessary to go into detail.

"I've known him for several years now. He's a good guy. I really like him."

"Yeah, I hear he's a very likable person." She hoped her sarcasm didn't come through. Everyone seemed to like Richard…first her mother and now Sylvia…

"Are you from Columbus?"

"No, I'm originally from Mississippi."

"Uh-uh!" Troy said in disbelief.

"Seriously, I am," she answered, disappointed to see the signal to cross the street. Whenever she was in a hurry, crosswalk signals took forever. Now that she wanted to take her time, the wait seemed to have accelerated.

"But you don't have an accent."

Natalie laughed. "Most people don't believe that I'm from the South, but I didn't move here until I was thirteen." She shrugged her shoulders. "I guess my accent faded over time. I know you can't be from here because you sound like you got a li'l bit of the country in you." She teased. They neared the spot where her red Camry was parked.

"Actually, I'm from Texas. I came up here to go to college and never left."

"This is my car," Natalie tried not to sound disappointed.

"So this is it, huh?" Troy looked down at her license plate. "Q T PIE…very clever…and correct," he looked at her with such intensity that she got butterflies.

"Thank you," she spoke softly.

"I hope this is not too forward of me, but I would like to call you sometime—if you'd give me your number."

"I would like that, too," she kept her eyes on him while reaching down into her purse for a pen and paper.

She hoped that giving him her work, home and cell numbers didn't make her look desperate. Troy didn't seem to mind. He placed the paper in his back pocket and said, "You'll be hearing from me…soon."

"I hope so," she deactivated the alarm on her car and Troy quickly stepped over to open the door for her.

Chapter 12

The Same Page

Friday afternoon Natalie stood in front of the vending machine in the break room trying to decide between the granola bar and the chocolate bar. Tonight she and Troy were going on their first date and Natalie couldn't wait. Though she wasn't looking to get into a serious relationship, Troy would certainly be a pleasant companion to have until she got ready to move back to New York.

"I see that someone is very happy today." Aneetra startled Natalie when she walked into the break room.

"Hey, what's up?" Natalie said and put her coins into the machine. She really wanted the chocolate, but since she had only been to the gym once this week, she settled for the granola bar instead.

"What were you standing there grinning about?"

"Nothing…I didn't even realize I was."

"Yeah—you were. You had a huge smile plastered all over your face. Is there some good news you would like to share?"

"No," Natalie avoided making eye contact and unwrapped her granola bar.

Aneetra put some change in the machine and got out a diet soda. "How's everything going with the house?" she asked, popping open her drink.

"Good. Lynn has had several inquiries, but no one has made an offer yet."

"Give it time. I'm sure all will go well." Aneetra sat down at one of the round tables in the room. "Are you staying in here?"

"No, I need to go make a phone call."

"Okay, I'm sure I'll talk to you later."

By the time Natalie got back to her desk, she'd already eaten her granola bar. She really didn't have a phone call to make. She'd just said that as an excuse to get away from Aneetra. It seemed like every time she was around that woman too long, she ended up sharing more information about herself than she wanted to. With several minutes of her break still left, and nothing else to do, Natalie pulled her cell phone out of her purse, and decided to call her grandmother.

"Hello?" Big Mama answered the phone.

"Hi, it's Natalie."

"Hey, baby."

"I'm on break, so I figured I'd give you a call now because I'm not gonna be home tonight."

"What do you have planned?"

"I'm just gonna hang out with a friend of mine," she answered vaguely, wanting to keep her date that evening private. Natalie had never been the type to bring her boyfriends home. With the exception of Bobby Kendall from high school, she had never introduced her mother to a single one of them, mainly because she assumed that her mother would not support her less-than-conventional relationships. Natalie's motives for getting involved with men had always fallen into the categories of either sex or money, sometimes both. Neither was likely to warrant parental approval, so she didn't even bother with formal introductions. Her interest in Troy had more to do with desiring companionship than wanting his money or sex...although the clearly defined muscles carved on his body made physical intimacy quite tempting. Still, Natalie didn't think loneliness was a good enough reason to tell her grandmother about him.

"I don't have anything planned for tonight," her grandmother added. "But, I'll be gone most of the day tomorrow to a women's retreat at the church. Um...I've been meaning to ask you somethin'."

"What is it?"

"It's been so long since I've seen you, I was wondering if you'd like to come down here for the Fourth of July."

Natalie felt the goose bumps sprout over her flesh. Going back to Mississippi wasn't something she was ready for. "Uh...I don't think I'll be able to take the time off work. I won't even be past my probation by then."

"Oh, okay. I want you to know you're always welcomed here. It doesn't have to be a holiday."

"Thanks. I appreciate that."

"I'm serious, Natalie."

"I believe you... Well, I'd better get off the phone and get back to work. I'll give you a call next week."

"Okay, I love you, baby."

"I—I love you, too."

Natalie and Troy's first date consisted of dinner and a movie. It was about a quarter to midnight when they pulled into the driveway outside her home. Troy turned off the ignition and they sat silently inside his black Lincoln Navigator for a moment.

"I had a nice time tonight," Troy spoke in a manner that tickled Natalie's stomach.

"I did, too. Would you like to come in?" She tried to sound casual about it, though the sensation beneath her stomach definitely cried out for them to do more than just hang out. As much as her body craved Troy's touch, she wasn't really trying to go there. Plus, it had been months since she'd gotten her birth control shot, so she needed to play it safe.

"I would love to come in," he said and followed her up the driveway to the house.

Natalie opened the door and flipped on the living room light, instructing him to have a seat while she went to the back. She assessed herself in the bedroom mirror. She had on the halter dress she'd gotten the other week at Nordstrom and was very pleased with how fresh her appearance looked after hours of being out. After spraying a mist of perfume, Natalie joined Troy on the living-room couch and asked, "Can I get you anything?"

"No, thank you."

"You could've turned the TV on."

"That's okay. I was hoping you would recite one of your poems to me."

"Not gonna happen."

"Why not? I thought it was interesting when you told me during dinner that you wrote poetry. The modeling didn't surprise me, but I would've never pictured you as a poet."

"And what does a poet look like?"

"I don't know. I didn't mean it as an insult, though. Can you at least tell me what kinds of things you write about?"

"Put it this way…I'm not one of those the sky-is-blue, grass-is-green poets. I write more about my life and feelings. Writing can be very therapeutic."

"Maybe I'll get to hear one of your poems before you pack up and move back to New York."

"We'll see. Enough about me…what else do you do besides lock up bad guys for a living?"

"Honestly, my two greatest hobbies are playing basketball and Xbox 360."

"Xbox?" Natalie scrunched her face. "Aren't you a little too old for that?"

Troy laughed. "Maybe it's the kid in me, but I love playing. You'll most likely find me kicked back on my couch playing a game than you would in a club…unless, of course, a pretty lady like yourself asked me to accompany her."

"Don't look at me. I haven't been to a club in a really long time. It starts to get old after a while."

"Yeah, I know what you mean. I partied hard in college and even for a while afterwards until my best friend started getting all religious on me and then moved to Chicago. Now I might go out with one of my friends from work every blue moon, but that's about it. Trust me, I'd rather be sitting here with you instead of with one of the fellas. You're much more pleasant to look at."

"Um-hmm. I bet you say that to all the ladies."

"No, just the ones I find special."

"Uh-oh, how many special ones have there been? I'm not gonna get jumped by a dozen baby mamas, am I?"

Troy laughed. "Not on my account. I don't have any kids."

"Whatever…"

"Why you say it like that?"

"Nowadays it's hard to find a brotha without children. I guess I just assumed…"

"Well, you're wrong. I'm not anyone's baby's daddy nor do I have any crazy ex-wives running around. I've never been married nor had children."

"How old are you again?"

"I just turned thirty-five in April."

"And you've *never* been married?"

"Nope." Troy's voice trailed off a bit when he answered.

She was skeptical about his response. She assumed that most men in their thirties had at least attempted to settle down even if the attempt had been unsuccessful. "I haven't been married either, but it's hard to believe that no woman has ever dragged you to the altar."

"That's probably what she would have to do—drag me. Getting married and starting a family is not for me. From what I can tell by watching others, both seem to complicate healthy relationships." He looked at Natalie with an awkward smile. "I think this is the point where you throw me out."

"For what?"

"Most women hear me say that and flip."

"Don't worry. I can relate to how you feel."

"You can?" Troy looked surprised.

"Yeah…I used to want to get married, but for all the wrong reasons. I guess I've never found my Mr. Right." Truthfully, Natalie had never been looking for him. She wasn't sure what qualities her Mr. Right would have—if he even existed. She'd never allowed herself to become emotionally involved enough even to explore the possibility.

"What were they?"

"What?"

"Your wrong reasons for wanting to get married."

Natalie shrugged her shoulders. Telling a guy she'd just met three days ago that she'd previously wanted to marry for money would likely send up a red flag. "Let's just say that after one very bad experience, marriage is no longer a priority of mine."

"It's good to know that we're on the same page," Troy gazed at her for a moment. Natalie could tell that he wanted to kiss her. "It's late. I'd better get going."

"I didn't know you had a curfew," she taunted.

"I don't. But, I'm trying to be a gentleman, and I'm not really sure I can be if I continue sitting here."

"What's that supposed to mean?" she asked, flirtatiously. Instead of answering her question, he leaned over and placed his warm soft lips over hers for the first time that night. Natalie squeezed her thighs together. If he made love anything like he kissed… She warned herself not to go there. She'd had impulsive sex with other men more times than she could recall and, in retrospect, the temporary pleasure didn't erase the deep-rooted emptiness in her soul. If anything, her sexual behavior added to it. Yet, no matter how much Natalie tried fighting her lust for Troy, her body continually responded to his kisses. One kiss led to another and before she knew it they were introducing each other to their birthday suits.

Chapter 13

A Standing Invitation

As Natalie waited for the elevator, she stood in the lobby thinking about Troy. They had been dating for about two months now. She didn't know what was becoming of their relationship, but she knew it went a lot deeper than just sex. There was something about him she found addictive. The only time she didn't think about him was when she was with him.

When Natalie finally got to her desk and logged onto her computer, she found a global e-mail message from Alex:

I'm sad to announce that Aneetra Bennett's mother, Joy Hughes, passed away over the weekend. Many of you know firsthand what a pleasure Aneetra is to work with. Those of us who have lost loved ones know that Aneetra has never failed to share an encouraging word with us. I ask that we now do something to let her know that we care and are saddened by her loss. Since none of us will likely attend the funeral service in Louisiana, I would like to send a floral arrangement to Aneetra and her family on behalf of all Dennison employees. If you would like to contribute please give your donations to Karen Tisdale or myself.

Having lost her own mother about six months ago, Natalie's heart ached for what Aneetra had to be going through. Immediately, she went down to Alex's office and donated money.

Aneetra was off work for two weeks. On the day she returned, Natalie walked over to Aneetra's cubicle and found her on the phone. "I'll come back later," she whispered, but Aneetra grabbed her arm and shook her head no. Natalie leaned against the partition and waited. She scanned all the computer-made scriptures hanging around her coworker's desk.

John 3:16 *For God so loved the world, that he gave his only begotten Son, that whosoever believeth in him should not perish, but have everlasting life.*
2 Timothy 1:7 *For God hath not given us the spirit of fear; but of power, and of love, and of a sound mind.*
1 John 4:4 ... *[G]reater is he that is in you, than he that is in the world.*

Aneetra seemed way too deep into the whole religion thing for Natalie, but Natalie couldn't explain why she was starting to like her or why she was even here at Aneetra's desk. They were complete opposites. Perhaps Natalie felt compelled to be there because of the incredible patience Aneetra seemed to have with her. Even when she brushed her off, Aneetra remained kind. Natalie had never met a friend like that before.

"I'll give you a call later on this week when I get them, and we'll talk then." Aneetra ended her call. "Hi, Natalie. Sorry about that."

"I just stopped by to see how you were doing. I'm really sorry to hear about your mother's death. I know what losing a mother feels like."

Aneetra reached out and squeezed her hand affectionately. "Thank you so much. It really means a lot to me to hear you say that. I appreciate your kindness."

"You're welcome…I won't stay. I know you probably have a lot of work to catch up on. I just wanted to welcome you back."

"Don't rush off. Tell me how things are going with you."

"Me? I'm doing fine."

"Have there been any new developments with the house? I spoke with Lynn when I was in Louisiana, but obviously I didn't think to ask her how things were going."

"Good. Lynn said that there's a couple who's really interested. She's working to get them financing. If all goes well, we should be able to close at the end of this month or sometime in September."

"Praise God!" Aneetra cheered. "That's great!"

Aneetra's excitement seemed unusual considering the circumstances. Natalie couldn't stop herself; she had to ask her about it. "How come you're so happy?"

"What do you mean?"

"I—I don't know. I don't mean to offend you. You just seem too carefree for someone whose mother passed away recently," she spoke, cautiously.

Aneetra gave a sly grin. "You didn't offend me at all. Actually it's a compliment."

"It is?"

"Yes. It shows that the joy of the Lord must really be working in me, because Natalie, I don't feel happy at all." Her smile quickly faded. "I'm hurting bad. It was a fight for me to get up and come into work this morning. I miss my mother *so* much. Truth be told, I'm a little mad because I think she got dealt a bad hand. During the years when she should've finally been able to enjoy her life, she dealt with one sickness after another." Natalie couldn't bear to look as Aneetra's eyes began to water. "But who am I to complain. She never did."

"I'm sorry…maybe I shouldn't have said anything,"

"No, don't be. It's wonderful that you think I'm handling it well, but make no mistake about it—what you see is the Lord working through me because I know if left on my own, I'd completely fall apart."

Natalie stood silent while Aneetra got a tissue off her desk and dabbed her eyes.

"Do you go to church?"

"I used to when I was little, but I don't anymore."

"You're more than welcome to come with my family and me anytime you'd like."

Natalie shook her head. "Thanks, but I'm not a church-going person."

Aneetra smiled. "I said that one time before, too."

Natalie sighed with relief when Aneetra's phone rang. All this church talk was getting to her for some reason. "I'm gonna let you get that. It might be important," she said.

"Thanks for coming by. Always remember you have a standing invitation to church with me whenever you want."

"Yeah…okay…"

Chapter 14

A Reason to Stay

From the living-room window Natalie could see the orange leaves being carried in the air by the wind. It was hard to believe October was already here. It seemed like only yesterday she'd lost her mother to breast cancer. At the time, Natalie hadn't thought she'd make it through, but somehow she had. Now she commemorated her mother's death by supporting the fundraisers held this month in honor of Breast Cancer Awareness, and proudly displayed a pink ribbon sticker on the back of her car's bumper.

Everything of her mother's that hadn't been bought during the garage sale had been donated to the Salvation Army, and now Natalie was in the process of getting her new place together. As a result of Lynn closing the deal on the house last month, Natalie had rented a two-bedroom ground-floor apartment in northern Columbus to be closer to her job. She was busy setting up her computer desk in the second bedroom when there was a knock at the door.

When Natalie looked out the peephole and saw Troy standing there, a bright smile spread across her face and her heart jumped. There was no way she was going to let him see her like this. "Just a sec…" she yelled, and raced across the hardwood floor to her bedroom, peeling off her cut-offs and ripped tie-dyed shirt. She threw on a pair of blue jeans and a polo shirt. Although she'd taken a shower earlier, she still applied some body spray to freshen up.

Troy knocked again.

"I'm coming…" She pulled her hair back into a ponytail as she raced to the door, almost tripping over one of her boxes.

"What took you so long?" He stood, smiling slyly with his hands behind his back.

Her heart fluttered at the sight of him. "Trust me, you didn't want to see how I looked."

"It's seeing a person at their worst that lets you know whether you *really* like them."

"Is that right?"

"Yeah, so you're gonna need to revert back to the way you were looking a few minutes ago if I'm gonna be able to make an accurate assessment of my feelings for you," he toyed.

"Whatever!" She simulated a stop sign with her right hand. "What are you doing here anyhow? I thought this was your Saturday to work."

"It was, but my buddy, Mitch, owed me a favor, and agreed to cover my shift. I wanted to come by and give you this." He pulled a box of candy and a small stuffed teddy bear from behind his back.

"Oh my gosh! Thank you! What did I do to deserve such a sweet gesture?"

"You didn't do anything." He kissed her on the forehead.

"I just happened to be out and decided to pick up something for you."

"Thank you." Natalie gave him a warm smile.

"You are very welcome." Troy brushed his lips across hers before walking completely into the apartment and hanging his jacket on the coatrack. "Did you have any plans for this evening?" he asked as they walked past her navy-blue velvet chaise to the couch.

"Nope…I was gonna try and finish getting the computer room together, then take a break and see if any good movies are on Lifetime." Natalie placed her gifts on the glass cocktail table.

Troy playfully rolled his eyes and sighed. "Is that the only channel females know how to find?" he teased. "You remind me of my mother and sister. They can watch Lifetime all day long."

"Hey, don't make fun of my channel. They have good movies, you know? For men *and* women. Maybe if you weren't so chauvinistic, you would've realized that by now," she kidded.

"Maybe if I hadn't been forced to watch a four-hour miniseries the time my keys mysteriously disappeared, I'd have more of an open mind." He was referring to an incident that had happened a while back when Natalie was still living in her mother's house. Troy had come over to help with the garage sale. Later that day, as Natalie was flipping through the television stations she came across a movie on Lifetime that she was interested in. Immediately, Troy assumed it was a chick flick and mentioned that he was going home to play his Xbox 360 for the remainder of the evening. But Natalie was enjoying his company and didn't want him to leave, so she hid his car keys. Troy was a good sport about the whole situation. At first, he searched around the house to see if he could find them, but then he gave up and sat through the rest of the movie for her sake.

"It's funny how your keys turned up after the movie, isn't it? I guess that's what happens when you're prejudiced like that…"

"How could you say something so hurtful?" He pretended to be on the verge of crying.

"Toughen up…" Natalie softly hit him in the arm.

Troy laughed as he pulled her closer to him. "I was really hoping that you would go somewhere with me. But, if you prefer to stay here and watch your precious network, then you'll miss out on spending the next two nights at Hocking Hills."

A bright smile crossed Natalie's face. Hocking Hills was located about an hour southeast of Columbus in Logan. She'd never been there, but she'd heard that the place was very secluded and a romantic spot. "I suppose I could accompany you."

"Oh no, don't bother…you just stay here and watch television. I had another female on reserve in case you couldn't make it," he joked.

Natalie pulled away and hit him hard this time.

"Ouch!" Troy rubbed his forearm where her fist had landed. "Why you gotta be so violent?"

"You better call and tell her to unpack her bags because I'll be the only woman you'll be spending the weekend with!"

"Well you better get packing."

She smiled at him again. "Give me fifteen minutes and I'll be ready." She gave him a peck before jumping up and going to her bedroom. "How long are we staying?" Natalie yelled out to him.

"'Til Monday morning, if that's all right with you," he hollered back. "There was a minimum two-night stay. We can leave early Monday morning—because I know you have to get back for work. I do, too."

"Okay." Natalie smiled, feeling like Cinderella being

whisked away by her prince. As much as she hated to admit it, she was developing real feelings for Troy. In a way, it scared her because she was used to keeping her heart out of relationships. She'd dated other men in the past that she'd liked, but none that she'd truly cared for. Things were different with Troy and she couldn't say for certain why that was.

Maybe he'd caught her at a vulnerable time in her life. There were absolutely no hidden agendas when they met. Natalie wasn't after his money, trying to break up a marriage or scheming to do anything she had done previously in other relationships. Yes, the sex was great, but that wasn't even the main attraction. He made her feel special and Natalie had allowed Troy to see a side of her that other men hadn't by sharing her most intimate feelings with him. She'd even broken down and recited one of her poems to him.

The five months they'd been together now had brought her a sense of security—something that she had never really had in previous relationships. Natalie had never let down her guard with men the way she had with Troy. When she was going through her mother's things, he was right there wiping her tears as she shared stories with him. Maybe Natalie had allowed Troy to get so close to her heart because she was in an emotionally weakened state after her mother's death. Perhaps she longed for the euphoria of experiencing true love similar to what she had heard in Sylvia's voice the night they'd talked about Richard. Whatever the reason, Natalie couldn't deny that she was falling hard for Troy.

In another week or so, she would be eligible to put in for a transfer to New York with Dennison. Though it would likely take a few months for the transfer to go through, she was having second thoughts about moving. She told Troy it was because she wanted to give herself more time to save. However, the truth was, she had plenty of money in her savings thanks to the sale of the house. She wasn't ready to leave him. Meeting Troy had given her a reason to stay around Columbus.

"I'm all set." She bounced into the living room with her luggage in hand. They were only going to be gone for two days and yet she had packed at least five days' worth of clothing, in addition to her intimate apparel. She doubted that she and Troy would be doing much sightseeing outside of their cabin, but she still wanted to make sure she had a variety of outfit choices available to her rather than being stuck wearing only one or two things. The fifteen minutes she'd promised had actually turned into about forty and Troy definitely took note.

"Maybe you misunderstood me…I said we'd only be gone for two days, not twenty," he teased.

"When you see my stash of Victoria's Secret goodies you're gonna wish it was the other way around."

"I bet I will…" he replied, passionately.

Chapter 15

Doctor Feel Good

Her head spinning like a top, Natalie jumped up and ran to the bathroom just in time for last night's dinner to make its way back up her esophagus and into the toilet. The strong wind pounding against the window did not make the situation any better. Rather, the noise seemed to magnify threefold in her head. The signs that winter was here had definitely appeared. The cold weather didn't bother Natalie, however, since her heart had been steadily warmed with the presence of Troy in her life.

What a way to start the New Year! she thought as her head hung over the commode. Today was January first, and based on the look of things, she would not be having a good day. Next month would mark the one-year anniversary of her mother's death. Back then it was as if her world had completely stopped. Thanks to Troy, it had begun rotating again. Although neither had uttered the words, Natalie knew that

Troy loved her just as much as she loved him. She could tell by his actions and the way he showered her with his attention and affection.

The difference between him and most other guys she'd dated was that it was clear that Troy wasn't in this relationship just for the physical pleasure. Though they were intimate the night of their first date, there were other occasions when they spent nights just talking and cuddling. Whenever they did make love, Natalie found it way more enjoyable with Troy than with any other man because she wasn't just spending time with him for money or for any other type of assistance. She was intimate with Troy because she loved being with him, and the more their relationship progressed, the more she opened her heart. Now he had full access, not only to her heart, but to her apartment as well, because she had given him a spare key—though most of the time he still knocked whenever he came by.

After involuntarily emptying the contents of her stomach, Natalie flushed the toilet and washed her face. She felt nauseated and her head hurt as though she had a hangover, except she hadn't been drinking last night. Natalie had brought the New Year in curled up on the couch under a blanket. She'd wished Troy was here, but he'd been in Houston for the last week visiting his family. She would have liked to have gone with him except Troy hadn't offered to take her along, and she hadn't asked.

Spending time alone this holiday season was difficult for Natalie because Christmas was her mother's favorite holiday. She missed the Christmas stockings that Sharon used to decorate, the eggnog that never tasted quite right and the selection of Christmas carols that her mother used to slaughter.

Though Natalie hadn't been to Mississippi in nearly two decades, she'd briefly considered going when Troy had announced he'd be in Houston for the holidays. Talking with her grandmother so much this year had brought back a deep longing to see her again, but ultimately Natalie wasn't sure if she could get over the apprehension about facing her past. As a desperate attempt to fight loneliness, she thought about calling over to Sylvia's house to see what her Christmas plans were. She changed her mind, assuming that somehow Sylvia's plans would involve Richard, and Natalie wasn't quite ready to spend the day with the two of them. She and Sylvia hadn't exactly become bosom buddies, but they did speak occasionally. Natalie had felt so isolated on Christmas day that she would've driven to Cleveland with Aneetra if she'd been invited.

The phone rang as Natalie was coming out of the bathroom and she hurried to answer it, hoping it was Troy, but one look at the caller ID proved her wrong.

"Happy New Year!" her grandmother said in a Southern drawl, sounding slightly different for some reason.

"Oh hey, Big Mama. Happy New Year to you, too."

"Were you expectin' someone else?"

"No, not really." She still hadn't told her grandmother about Troy.

"What do you plan on doin' today?"

"I don't know. I'll probably stay in. I don't feel too good."

"It might be that ol' flu bug goin' around. You ain't got no fevah do you?"

Natalie put the back of her hand on her forehead. "No, I don't think so. Something I ate last night must've not agreed with me."

"Make sure you get some rest."

"That's what I plan to do."

"I'm goin' over to Toni's. She called right before I called you and said she would be here in about a half hour to get me. I wanted to call you now 'cuz I'll probably be over there the whole day. Last night I told her I would help her finish cookin' before everyone got over there. I guess I better get off the phone and finish gettin' ready or else she'll be fussin' when she gets here. I still gotta put my teeth in and do somethin' with my hair."

Natalie couldn't help but laugh. That explained her grandmother's odd speech. "Well you go do what you need to do and I'll talk to you another time."

"Okay, honey, I hope you feel better."

"Thanks, I'm sure I will."

"All right then, I love you."

"I know—I love you, too." Within minutes of hanging up the phone, it rang again. "Happy New Year!"

"Hey, babe…" Troy sounded as though he was still half asleep.

"I see someone did a li'l too much partying last night."

"If that's what you call being at the emergency room until two in the morning…."

"Emergency room! What happened? Are you all right?"

"Yeah, I'm fine. I went with my sister to take my nephew. He had a fever of a hundred and three."

"What's wrong with him?"

"He's got a bad case of the flu. My sister is just like my mom—she freaks out whenever one of her kids gets sick. Lucky I was here because the two of them acted like they were going to have a nervous breakdown. The doctor prescribed some medicine and said that he should be all right. We're just keeping a close eye on him."

"Well I hope he feels better. I'm not feelin' too good myself."

"And you accused me of partying?"

"Whatever…I don't know what's wrong with me. Something I ate last night didn't agree with me."

"Well you better get it together because I'm still going to need you to pick me up from the airport. That is, of course, if you want to see me."

"You're talkin' crazy now…"

Troy laughed. "Seriously though, the flu is going around."

"Yeah, that's what my grandmother said."

"Maybe you should go and get checked out at urgent care or something just to be on the safe side."

"Urgent care is probably packed around this time of the year. I'll just wait and see how I feel in a few days. Besides, the only doctor I'm anxious to see is my personal Doctor Feel Good. You're the only one who can make me feel like a natural woman again."

"Okay, Aretha Franklin. Why are you starting stuff you can't back up over the phone? I should probably get off the phone and spend time with my family since it's my last day and all. I'll call you tomorrow before I go to the airport."

"All right…have a safe flight."

"I plan to. Happy New Year, again."

"The same to you." One more day! She couldn't wait to see Troy tomorrow. Still feeling a little woozy, Natalie decided to lie back down. It wasn't long before she was rushing off to the bathroom again. After going through this scenario several more times, Natalie was thankful that she had stayed put for the holidays. There was no better place for her to feel crappy than in the comfort of her own home.

Chapter 16

A Thin Line

Natalie walked into her apartment, threw her keys and purse on the coffee table while tossing her coat on the back of the chaise, and plopped down on the couch. She couldn't wait until Troy got off work. She hated when he worked on Saturdays. Today more than ever, time seemed to be her enemy as it crept by, not caring that she was anxious to talk to him. She thought about calling his cell phone, but figured it would be better to tell him in person. He'd returned from Texas a few weeks ago, and Natalie had continued going through bouts of sickness. At first, she'd thought it was the flu, but the tender breasts, nausea and headaches were all too familiar, and she began to suspect otherwise. A missed menstrual cycle and a positive diagnosis from an obstetrician confirmed that her ailment had nothing to do with influenza.

"I'm going to be a mother…" Natalie smiled and whispered out loud as the reality of her situation sank in. Initially, she'd been stunned by the news and wondered if she would have what it took to be a good mother. Would she be able to prevent her child from experiencing the heartache she'd gone through during her childhood? She'd never been around any babies longer than a couple of hours; would she know how to care for one properly? Though there were other aspects of motherhood that caused Natalie some concern, she couldn't help but feel an instantaneous love for her unborn child. Considering children were never part of her plans, Natalie was more excited than she'd ever thought she'd be. She pledged to do her very best to love and care for the baby. What she didn't know about motherhood, she was willing to learn.

It wouldn't be long before her flat abdomen stretched out beyond recognition. The doctor had estimated that she was about six weeks pregnant, and had written her out a prescription for prenatal vitamins, which she'd filled before coming home. The stapled paper bag from the pharmacy rested in her purse. Eventually she would tell her grandmother about the pregnancy. Right now, she was more eager to talk to Troy. She suspected Troy would be excited about the baby as well since their relationship had evolved to the point where it seemed like they would be together forever.

The minutes seemed like hours as Natalie listened to the slow tick of the wall clock. It would still be several hours before she saw Troy. He didn't get off until four. Natalie carelessly flipped through the channels with the remote. Nothing sparked her interest long enough to hasten time—not even the movie playing on her favorite network or the special showing of *Steel Magnolias* on another channel. With impatience brewing inside, Natalie needed some way to keep busy until Troy got off. With the baby consuming her thoughts, she headed back out the door, deciding to kill time by window-shopping at the place where she assumed she'd be spending at lot of time over the next several months.

Natalie strutted into Babies "R" Us with excitement. The store was crowded with expectant mothers strolling through the aisles. Even in a place filled with hundreds of others, Natalie felt alone because she didn't have anyone to shop with as the other women did. "Things won't be like this forever," she whispered to herself as reassurance. Once Troy found out about the baby, she suspected it wouldn't be long before they married. It didn't matter to her if they did it before or after the expected due date in September. The bottom line was that eventually she, Troy and the baby would be a family.

Natalie spent the next hour looking at everything from newborn clothing, cribs, diapers, bottles and other baby accessories. She was overwhelmed by the variations of each item. For instance, there weren't just plain old baby bottles. There were easy-grip bottles, wide-neck bottles, medium-flow bottles, fast-flow bottles, bottles with flat silicone nipples, bottles with round silicone nipples and the list went on and on. She hadn't a clue which ones, if any, were better. With so many choices, Natalie resolved right then and there to breast-feed. At least both of her breasts were just alike and she wouldn't have to confuse herself—or the baby—with all the different bottle options.

Having a baby was definitely going to force her to make plenty of adjustments in her life. If she was having trouble picking a bottle, Natalie could only imagine the headaches she would put herself through when it came to finding child-care. Would she even be able to trust the care of her baby to anyone else? Troy made a pretty decent income, so maybe he would be supportive of her staying home with the baby. There were so many decisions that she would have to make and she wondered if she would be able to fully grasp this thing called motherhood. Despite her fears about parenting, she was comforted by the belief that things would be different this time. She was having this child with someone she truly cared for and who she knew cared for her. With Troy by her side, she was sure that everything concerning their baby would be just fine.

When Natalie's phone rang, she didn't have to look at the caller ID to know it was Troy. She'd programmed a special ring tone just for him. "Hello," she said, trying to contain her zeal.

"Hey, where're you at? I tried calling your apartment."

"Oh, um…I'm at the store. I got bored sitting around there and wanted to get out."

"Are we still on for this evening?"

"Of course we are."

"Do you wanna catch a movie tonight?"

"Naw…let's stay in. A good movie is coming on Lifetime that I would love to see. I was hoping you would watch it with me."

"No, thanks. I'd rather watch the weather channel."

"I was just playing. Why don't we rent a movie instead?"

"That's cool. Anything in particular you want to see? I'll stop and get one on my way over."

"No, you just hurry yourself up. I'll get the movie. I'm on my way home anyhow."

"All right then. Have you eaten?"

"Earlier."

"I'm in the mood for Chinese, you want some?"

"Uh-uh. Can you just pick me up a veggie sub from somewhere or something else light?" She didn't know if she'd be able to handle a heavy meal on her stomach.

"Yeah, I can do that. Well, I gotta wrap up some paper work before I can get out of here. I'll see you in a little while."

Eager to get home, she proceeded down the aisle consumed with thoughts of exactly how and at what point during the evening she would share the news with Troy. She turned the corner of the aisle so quickly that she bumped into the end of a cart.

"Oh excuse m—" Natalie's words wedged in her throat as two familiar pairs of eyes looked her way. Standing at the other end of the shopping cart were Wendy and her sister, Kim. "Hi…" Natalie said softly as her former friend stared blankly.

Suddenly, her excitement about Troy and the baby diminished and shame took its place. Natalie tensed up as she expected Wendy to have a few choice words to share. To her surprise, both women threw her a greeting and continued down the aisle as if she had been a complete stranger.

"Wendy…" Natalie called out before she could stop herself.

"Yes." Her former friend turned and answered in a calm, but alert manner.

"Look…I know that you probably didn't expect or want to see me again, but for what it is worth, I'm sorry."

"Apology accepted."

Things had gone more smoothly than Natalie had thought they would and she sighed with relief. Why shouldn't she apologize? What she had done was wrong. Besides, the situation with Kevin didn't matter anymore. She no longer wanted him; she had Troy. "How have you been?"

"I'll be in the next aisle when you finish," Kim said to her sister. Her leaving was probably a good thing. Natalie had had an encounter with her once before, and knew Kim wasn't one to hold her tongue.

"I'm sure you never expected to see me in a place like this, but I just found out today that I'm six weeks pregnant," she announced. Okay, so Wendy wasn't exactly the first person she wanted to share her news with considering that she had once gone after the woman's husband, but sometimes things happened. "I see I'm not the only one expecting."

"Natalie, I accepted your apology, but I think you need

to be clear as to what that means." Wendy spoke in a very even tone and a polite manner. "First of all, I forgive you. It wasn't easy, but I *had* to for the sake of my own relationship with God. Forgiveness does not mean that we are friends. I can no longer trust you. Experience has taught me that unfortunately, there can be a very thin line between friend and foe. With that said, congratulations on your pregnancy, and please, have a wonderful day." Without saying another word, Wendy turned and walked away.

Oh well… Natalie thought to herself, *at least I tried.*

Chapter 17

Point of No Return

Troy showed up at her place just a few minutes after six, and Natalie immediately wrapped her arms around his neck.

"Hey, slow your roll," Troy teased while trying not to drop the food from his hands. "You're acting like you missed me or something."

"I have missed you. I've been going crazy all day waiting for you to get here."

He gave her a gentle peck on the lips. "I missed you, too, but can we finish this conversation after we eat, because I'm starvin'?"

"I suppose…" Natalie said flippantly before letting go of him.

Troy barely said another word until after he'd devoured his chicken chow mein. Natalie ate bits and pieces of her sub. Although she had been hungry earlier, seeing Troy and the anticipation of telling him about the baby were enough to make her lose her appetite. Once they'd finished eating, Troy picked up where he had left off, giving Natalie a much more intense kiss.

She thought now would be the perfect time to tell him about the baby. She had originally planned to wait until after they had watched the movie, but they hadn't even gotten to that yet, and the enthusiasm was eating away at her. "I have something to tell you," she managed to say as Troy gently kissed her neck.

"What is it?" he mumbled without looking up.

"I…went…somewhere today."

"Um-hmm." Natalie knew he was barely listening. By now his hands were slithering up and down her body.

She was quickly losing focus, and her emotions were taking control. She was just as eager as he was to make love, but first she needed to inform him of their wonderful news. "I had a doctor's…appointment this morning."

"Um-hmm…"

"And I…found out…that we are…going to be parents."

"What!" Troy halted his activities and sat straight up.

"I'm six weeks pregnant." Natalie's huge smile felt as though it consumed her entire face.

Troy had a solemn look in his eyes. "You're not seriously thinking about having the baby, are you?"

It wasn't the reaction Natalie had expected. Perhaps he was scared. That would be understandable. After all, she was initially a little nervous as well, too. Maybe if she expressed her fears she could calm his in the process. "I know…it's definitely unexpected. At first, I was scared, too. I mean, let's be real, we've only been together less than a year, we're not married, and I haven't even met your parents. But the more I thought about it, the more I believe it's fate. We are perfect for each other, and I just know that everything will be fine." She leaned over on his shoulder and rubbed his chest to assure him.

Troy's body went rigid as a corpse. "I don't want children," he whispered.

This wasn't really how things were supposed to go. He was supposed to embrace the idea of becoming a father, rub her belly and wish for a little boy. He was supposed to kiss her and tell her how much he loved her. Maybe he would even hint around to the two of them spending the rest of their lives together. Then they would physically express their excitement about the baby by repeatedly making love throughout the night. Things weren't going the way she had scripted, and it was making her nervous. "What are you saying?" she quivered.

"I'm saying that I *don't* want you to have the baby." He looked her dead in the eyes. "There are many places to get abortions around here."

"Abortion? You want me to have an abortion?" The thought hadn't even crossed her mind. How could he suggest such a thing!

"I think that would be best." He spoke matter-of-factly.

"Best for whom? I don't understand…. I thought we had a great thing going."

"We do…"

"I assumed that eventually you would ask me to marry you and then—"

"Please don't say you got pregnant on purpose because you wanted to get married." He threw his head back and sighed in despair.

"I didn't! But are you saying that you have no intentions of marrying me?"

"Look…I think you are a great person…and I really, really like you and all—"

"But—" Natalie's emotions ran the gamut of hurt, confusion and anger. Like a mother who had just heard that her young child had been killed in a drive-by shooting, Natalie's heart pleaded for the messenger to have mercy and some-how transform the message of despair into one of delight. However, his professional training and his thirteen years in law enforcement had given Troy the ability to deliver unpleasant news without allowing his emotions to get in the way, and he did just that.

"Getting married and starting a family have never been goals of mine. We talked about this the very first night we went out. You said you understood where I was coming from."

"We didn't know each other back then, Troy. Of course, I would say that. I had just met you. I didn't know our relationship would evolve to this, and neither did you, which is why I suspected you'd said what you did."

"Natalie, I meant everything I said. Not because I didn't know you. I've felt this way for a long time."

His words were strong enough to kill. Rather than a child, it was Natalie's dream of them being a family that had been laid to rest. She really wanted this baby. No explanation would be good enough to justify the senseless death of a child. Likewise, nothing Troy said would excuse the fact that he had killed her dream unnecessarily, unjustly and while it was still undeveloped. Maybe if he knew about the things that had happened in her past he would be more sympathetic. Maybe…but Natalie couldn't tell him about that. She'd never told anyone.

"In my line of work, the chances of a successful or long-standing marriage are slim to none. The majority of law-enforcement officers are divorced, separated or unhappily married with children. I go to work each and every day not knowing whether I'll be alive by the end of the shift. That's enough pressure in and of itself! I don't want the added stress of knowing that if I die, I'm leaving behind a wife and child."

"What would be the difference between that and leaving behind a girlfriend?"

"I don't know…it's just different."

"I don't understand, Troy. You've made me feel so special these last seven months, surprising me with romantic dinners, weekend trips and flowers at work. What was it all for—just because I'm good in bed?"

"No! I swear, it's more than that. I really like you."

"Do you love me?"

"Natalie—"

"Don't Natalie me, answer the question. *Do you love me?*"

"Listen, baby, I can tell that you're upset. Can we both calm down and talk about this later?" He tried to put his arm around her, but Natalie pulled away.

"Get out, you selfish jerk!" She stood up and pointed toward the door.

"Nat, I think you're overreacting—"

"Get out, Troy!" she yelled as warm tears poured down her cheeks.

"Baby—" he unsuccessfully tried gently tugging her back down to him. "I don't want to leave on such a sour note."

"Too late for that," she folded her arms, and rolled her eyes. Tonight their relationship had been severely damaged, possibly to the point of no return.

Troy got up and grabbed Natalie's shoulders, tenderly. He forced eye contact with her and she didn't have the strength to pull away this time. "I'm gonna respect your wishes and leave, but kicking me out isn't going to solve anything. We're still gonna have to talk about this."

"Just get out of my face…"

"I'll give you a call tomorrow."

"Don't bother."

Troy looked as though he wanted to say something else, but instead he got his jacket and left. Natalie collapsed on the couch, bawling because her heart had been ripped into pieces.

Chapter 18

Vice Versa

In the weeks following her argument with Troy, Natalie tried hard to keep up a front by pretending all was well in her life whenever she talked to her grandmother on the phone or saw Aneetra at work. Both women had asked Natalie on several occasions if everything was all right with her. A resounding No! screamed from the depths of her soul, but she couldn't bring herself to say that to either of them. It seemed easier to hide her distress from her grandmother because all she had to do was make sure it didn't show in her voice. However, when Aneetra was around, Natalie also had to be careful not to let her agony show on her face.

Things had simmered down a bit between her and Troy. Technically they were still a couple, but the nature of their relationship had changed drastically. Hanging out with Troy used to be fun, but now it was awkward because there was still no consensus about the pregnancy. Since they couldn't avoid arguing whenever the subject came up, they really didn't talk about it much. Natalie just couldn't bring herself to have an abortion, nor could she give up on the idea of her, Troy and the baby being a family. Somehow she would find a way to convince Troy to change his mind. Any other outcome was much too devastating to think about.

"Hey, Natalie. I'm leaving my apartment right now," Troy called her on his cell phone the minute he hopped into his Navigator.

"Okay, everything is ready," she sang.

Troy smiled. She sounded happy. He hoped that celebrating Valentine's Day tonight would rekindle the fire they'd once had. This pregnancy had definitely put a strain on their relationship. He wished everything could return to normal between them—how it was before the baby had intruded on their lives.

He didn't understand why Natalie had been so adamant about having the child. He'd thought they'd been in agreement about not getting married and having children when they met. Somewhere down the line, she'd changed positions on him. He should've seen it coming. He'd dated other women who seemed initially to be okay with the idea that there would be no long-term commitment, then they'd switch gears as time progressed.

Luckily none of those women had ever gotten pregnant by him so he could truly walk away from those relationships with no strings attached. He couldn't do that with Natalie. Not just because of the baby, but because there was something special about her. Troy really liked her. Not only was her smile beautiful, but she was such a carefree, fun-loving person and he enjoyed spending time with her. How could he make her understand that having this baby was something she couldn't do? He was never meant to be a father.

Troy got to Natalie's apartment about a quarter after seven and knocked on the door. His stomach growled from the pleasing aroma of her cooking. He'd wanted to take her out to a nice restaurant, but she'd insisted that he come over and that she cook dinner.

"Hey, there," Natalie answered the door, smiling.

Troy's eyes scanned her from head to toe. Her hair hung over her shoulders and she was dressed in a long, fiery-red, see-through nightgown. He hoped she'd be what he was having for dessert. It had been a while since they had been intimate. "You look hot," he said, bringing his eyes back up to hers.

"Thank you. You don't look too bad yourself."

Troy quickly examined his black dress pants. His long-sleeved, hunter-green shirt was hidden underneath his jacket. "I feel a bit overdressed," he teased.

"I'm sure we can take care of that before the end of the night," Natalie backed away from the door to allow him entry into the apartment.

Once inside, Troy took his coat off, hanging it on the nearby rack. Natalie wrapped her arms around his neck, and kissed him with such intensity that she sparked a physical reaction. "Happy Valentine's Day," she whispered before letting go.

"You, too," he gently grabbed her arm, wanting more of her. "I didn't expect you to answer the door dressed like that." He pulled her closer, forcing her arms back around him.

"I hope it was a pleasant surprise."

"Of course it was. Why do you think I don't want to let you go?" He leaned down and pressed his lips against hers. Once again, their tongues tangled and he was ready to skip dinner, and go straight for dessert.

Natalie pulled away again, grinning from ear to ear. Troy smiled, too. He hadn't seen such a happy expression on her face in weeks. "I hope you're hungry," she said, taking him by the hand and leading him into the kitchen.

Troy surveyed the small round dining table. The glass tabletop was covered with a red cloth and decorated with two wineglasses, a bottle of sparkling grape juice and two candles: one red and the other white. The roll of paper towels had been moved to the counter and replaced with white folded napkins which rested underneath the silverware.

"Have a seat…"

He did so, and she brought over their plates. His mouth watered when he saw the juicy T-bone steak, mashed potatoes with gravy, steamed vegetables and buttermilk biscuits which had delighted his nostrils at the door. "This is nice," he said, watching her dim the lights and ignite both candles. Natalie didn't say a word. She continued smiling and took her seat across from him.

Troy cut into his tender steak. He took his first bite of the perfectly seasoned meat. "*De*-licious!" he said.

"Thank you."

There wasn't much conversation while the two were eating. Troy could not get over how gorgeous Natalie looked tonight or how well things seemed to be going with them. Natalie seemed like a different person. Maybe she'd finally realized that their lives would be less complicated without the pitter-patter of little feet.

Stretched out in her bed, Natalie absorbed the comfort of Troy's arms. Her head lay on his chest, and she could hear every thump his heart made; she'd swear it was in sync with hers. So far, everything had gone just as she'd planned. They'd shared a wonderful meal and then they'd made love amidst the yellow-orange glow of the candlelight, compensating for the drought they'd experienced the last three and a half weeks. "Do you have to work tomorrow?" she looked up, her lips inches away from his.

"Unfortunately, I do." He lifted his head just high enough

to brush his mouth across hers, and then lay back down. "I had a wonderful time tonight. We really needed this."

"I know." Natalie lowered her head to his and their lips came together once again. "Why don't you stay the night?"

Natalie's eyes followed Troy's when he turned toward the clock. It was 10:27 p.m. "I would, but I didn't bring my work clothes with me. Had I known things would go like this, I would've because I'm definitely not in a hurry to leave."

Natalie smiled and laid her head back on his chest, circling through his chest hair with her index finger. "Wouldn't it be great if we could spend every night like this?"

Troy squeezed her gently, "Yes, it would."

"I've been thinking…what if we moved in together? Maybe I could find someone to take over my apartment and move into yours since it's bigger."

"I don't know, baby. I haven't lived with anyone since I was in college. I'm sort of set in my ways now. Besides, having two separate places adds a little more excitement, don't you think? We're not stuck in one spot. If we get tired of hanging out here, we can go to my crib, and vice versa."

That wasn't the answer Natalie wanted to hear, and so she continued to press her case. "I see what you're saying, but I just thought maybe you would enjoy having home-cooked meals on a daily basis. I know you eat out a lot. With me there, you could save money on food *and* save on gas from not driving over here all the time. Spending the night wouldn't be an issue anymore. We could spend all our nights like this and not have to worry about whether or not we brought over our work clothes."

Troy lifted her head up so he could see her eyes. "What is this really about, Natalie?" He asked softly. "You've never mentioned us moving in together before. Why now, all of a sudden?"

"I don't know. I just thought maybe it would help. Our

relationship has been so tense lately. Maybe if we moved in together, things would be different." She started to look down, but Troy grabbed and held on to her chin, looking at her softly.

"Listen to me. We don't have to force ourselves into a living arrangement just to hang on to our relationship. Things have been difficult the last few weeks, but we'll get through this together, I promise."

"Are you saying what I think you're saying?" Natalie was about to get excited until she saw Troy's confused expression. She lowered her voice and spoke nervously, "You haven't changed your mind about the baby, have you?" She smacked his hand from under her chin, and jumped out of bed, searching for her robe.

"Natalie, wait!" Troy said, bouncing up, and slipping on his pants.

"Just leave me alone! I can't believe you're willing to abandon me. I didn't make this baby by myself, you know?"

"Whoa, sweetheart!" He grabbed her, holding tight. "I would never abandon you. Trust me. I do accept responsibility for this mess we're in. You're not in this alone. We should have been more care—"

"How can you say that?"

"Say what?"

"You accept responsibility for this mess we're in. We didn't fall into the mud, Troy. I'm nine weeks pregnant. It's not a mess! It's our baby!" she screamed, beating her fist into his chest several times until he caught her hands.

"I'm sorry I said that. Just calm down." He brought her close to him.

Tears rolled down her cheeks. "I tried so hard to make tonight perfect."

"It was, baby," he reassured her, gently swiping the hair from around her face.

"I don't understand. Why can't you see that we're good together? I love you so much, Troy. This baby is important to me. I can't have an abortion. I just can't," she sobbed, remembering how difficult it had been the last time she had forfeited her rights to motherhood.

"Okay..." he sounded defeated.

"Why don't you want the baby?"

"Nat—it's difficult for me to explain. I'm not ready for this. Being a father wasn't something I'd planned for my life."

"It's not like I planned this either."

Troy sighed, "I know."

"Just leave me alone. I won't force you to become a part of the baby's life. I promise not to list you on the birth certificate."

"Do you think that's going to make me feel better?"

"Why not? You don't want anything to do with this child."

"I don't want you to have the baby, but if you do, I'll take care of my responsibility. I can't walk away with a good conscience."

"So it's your conscience keeping you in the situation rather than love for me or our child?"

Troy breathed heavily and tilted his head up toward the ceiling. "Must you nitpick at everything I say? I'm done talking about this tonight. We're not accomplishing anything!" He grabbed his shirt and stormed out of the room, extinguishing one of the candles as he flew by it.

Chapter 19

Far from Perfect

The next day, Natalie found it impossible to concentrate at work. She couldn't call in sick, though. Yesterday she'd promised to have a major report ready for Alex by three today and it was already eleven-thirty. Although she'd planned to skip lunch, at the rate she was going, she still wouldn't finish on time. "This is Natalie," she answered when her work phone rang.

"Hey..." It was Troy.

"Hey..." she repeated softly.

"I won't hold you long. I just called to say I'm sorry for leaving the way I did last night."

"Thanks, but your walking out is the last thing concerning me. I don't get your attitude, Troy. If I was some one-night stand who'd ended up pregnant—then I could see why you feel the way you do, but I don't get it. I really don't. You act like having this child with me is one of the worst things that could happen to you."

"Look, this is not the time for us to get into any heavy discussions. You want to have the baby and that's that. I'll do what I need to do, all right?"

"You act as if we're making a business deal…"

"Bye, Natalie. I'm not going through this with you again. I'll give you a call later, okay?"

"Jerk!" she sputtered, slamming the phone down.

"I suppose you're gonna tell me that nothing's wrong?"

Natalie jumped at the sound of Aneetra's voice. "Why are you sneaking up behind me?"

"I didn't sneak, I came to drop off the budget analysis for the Carson account. You're submitting the final report to Alex, right?"

"Yeah…" Natalie stared at her computer, refusing to turn Aneetra's way.

Aneetra laid a manila folder on her desk. "If you have any questions, let me know."

"Okay."

"Natalie…"

"What?"

"I don't mean to pry, but you've seemed very upset about something lately. What just happened now is proof of that. I'm willing to listen if there's something you want to talk about."

"Thanks, Aneetra, but what's happening in my life is something you wouldn't be able to relate to."

"And how would you know that?"

"Because your life is perfect." Aneetra was a happily married mother of two and, with the exception of her mother dying, the major crises in her life were probably things like deciding what she'd fix her family for dinner. As far as Natalie was concerned, Aneetra's issues were very minor compared to the situations she had encountered during her lifetime and the one she was currently facing.

Aneetra laughed sarcastically. "My life is *far* from perfect." She took her normal seat at the corner of Natalie's desk.

Natalie desperately wished Aneetra would leave her alone because she could not trust herself around this woman, fearing that somehow Aneetra would trick her into exposing her vulnerability. Tears were already starting to well up in her eyes. She quickly grabbed a tissue to blot them dry.

"Have you taken lunch yet?"

Natalie shook her head. "I won't be able to. I have to finish this report."

"Oh don't worry about the report. I'll help you finish it after lunch."

"Thanks, but I'm fine…really," Natalie argued.

"No, you're not…really," Aneetra mocked, sparking a slight grin from Natalie. "Now, you can either come to lunch with me or sit here and draw attention to yourself. Ain't no telling who's watching or got their ears perked up. You know how people love to get rumors started around this place. So what's it gonna be? Are you coming to lunch or are you gonna sit here and let the whole office see you cry?"

"I'm not really hungry," Natalie continued to protest.

"That's fine. We don't have to leave the building. I would say we could go to the break room, but too many people will be in and out of there this time of day. We can always go hang out in one of the back conference rooms and talk. I doubt anyone's using it now."

Natalie looked up at Aneetra for the first time since she'd been at her desk. "You're not gonna leave unless I say yes, are you?"

"Nope," Aneetra smiled.

"Fine," she said, grabbing her purse.

Aneetra was right; no one was using the conference room. Attached to its sky-blue-painted walls were a white board, a projection screen, and wooden plaques revealing bits of Dennison history, such as the date the company was established, its mission and a chronological list of company presidents through the years. A rectangular table sat directly in the center, stretching nearly the entire length of the room. Natalie got a glimpse of the cars passing by as she glanced out the ceiling-to-floor, wall-to-wall window along the back, which overlooked the I-270 outerbelt. "Will we get in trouble for being in here?" she asked, having never been in the conference room unless attending an actual meeting.

"Get in trouble?" Aneetra frowned, shutting the door. "Haven't you noticed by now how laid-back this place is? No one gets in trouble for anything. The three main reasons anyone will get reprimanded is for falsifying work hours, sending inappropriate e-mails or tampering with confidential information—and in that case a person is likely to get fired. Don't worry, using the conference room is not a violation of any office policy."

Natalie took a seat at the table, wondering if there was any believable story she could concoct to keep from telling Aneetra what was really going on.

"So—what's been bothering you the last few weeks?"

"I don't know…you're not gonna understand. We are so different, Aneetra."

"Is this about my life being perfect again?"

"It sure seems that way to me. You come to work every day with a smile, no matter what happens. Even when your mother died you still seemed happy. I mean, in reality, I know nothing's perfect, but your life seems pretty close."

"All I can say is that it's not. I choose to smile every day, but I don't always feel like doing so."

"Still, I'm sure you don't know how it feels to be pregnant by a guy who wishes you would have an abortion." Natalie hung her head, wondering how in the world she had let that slip out. This pregnancy combined with the stress of her relationship with Troy was surely messing with her emotions. She did not need to be around Aneetra in such a fragile state of mind because the woman had a way of getting her to talk about things that she wouldn't normally reveal.

"That certainly explains why you've been so edgy lately. What have you decided to do?"

"I really don't know," Natalie admitted, her voice shaking. "It's a no-win situation. I really want to keep the baby, but if I do, I'll push Troy further away."

"Why does he want you to have an abortion?"

"He says it's because he never planned to have kids." Natalie began to tear up again, but took several deep breaths to prevent from doing so. "I just don't understand. Our relationship was great. I thought he'd be happy about the baby, but…maybe he's right. Maybe it would be best if I had an abortion."

"I'd think long and hard before doing that. Abortion is permanent. Once it's done, it's done, and there's no turning back."

Natalie nodded her head in agreement. She already knew the ramifications she faced.

"I know someone who had an abortion in college. She's married now with children, but to this day, she's still haunted by her decision."

"I just don't know what to do. I want to be with Troy, I just want him to be happy about the baby. His attitude is stressing me out. I thought we had a good relationship. I feel so stupid."

"I know exactly how you feel."

Natalie looked up skeptically.

"I can…the woman I told you about was me."

"*You* had an abortion?"

Aneetra nodded. "Fifteen years ago. I was nineteen at the time—in the middle of my sophomore year. I got knocked up by my boyfriend who made it known that he would deny the baby if I went through with the pregnancy."

"Really?"

"Yep. And to make matters worse, I found out that he'd gotten another girl on campus pregnant, too. Imagine going home and explaining all of that to your mama.… Not only didn't I want to face my mama, but I was concerned about what my friends would think. I felt like a complete fool. Pride got the best of me and I did the only thing I thought I could do at the time."

Natalie shook her head in disbelief. "I never would've thought—you're so religious."

"I cringe when people use that word to describe me."

"Why? It's true."

"Yeah, but there are a lot of religious people in the world who haven't necessarily given their lives to Christ. There *is* a difference. One is a systematic way of doing things, but salvation is a life-changing experience."

Great! Now Aneetra was getting all evangelical…

"I got saved a few years after I'd had my abortion. I know that Jesus instantly forgave me then, but it took much longer for me to forgive myself. I can't tell you what to do about your pregnancy, but remember that you have to live with whatever decision you make."

"Thanks…I'm sure I'll figure this whole thing out soon. Will you promise me something?"

"What?"

"Please don't say anything about my situation to anyone. I'd prefer to keep my personal life separate from work."

"Girl, you don't have to worry about that. I won't tell anyone."

"Good. I won't say anything about what you've told me, either."

"I guess we have a deal then, huh?"

Natalie smiled. "I guess so." Talking to Aneetra hadn't been all that bad. Having kept secrets from everyone for most of her life, it felt good to share something for once.

"Now, I think we better get back so we can finish the Carson report. Alex is cool, but you don't want to get on her bad side. However, before we leave, would you mind if I prayed with you?"

"Sure, why not?"

Aneetra began, "Father God, I come to You on behalf of Natalie, who is going through a tough time right now. Lord, she is in need of Your strength and guidance, and so I ask that You speak to her heart. Replace fear with faith and give her wisdom to make the choices that coincide with Your will for her life. Only You know the depths of her pain and I ask, in the Name of Jesus, that You heal her every hurt. Show her Your loving kindness…"

Natalie listened intently as Aneetra's prayer brought tears to her eyes. Besides her grandmother, she had never heard anyone pray so fervently on her behalf. She was thankful that her life's path had crossed with Aneetra's, and that Aneetra had continued pursuing her friendship even when she behaved in a less-than-friendly manner. That day in the conference room, Natalie began to see Aneetra in a whole new light. Once irritated by her offers, she now appreciated the fact that Aneetra cared enough about her to pray for her. Natalie still wasn't certain about how the whole situation with her, Troy and the baby would work out. But she did know that, at least for the moment, she felt better and she was sure it was a direct result of the words leaving her friend's lips and landing in God's ears.

Chapter 20

The Waiting Game

The short, auburn-haired nurse rested her chubby hand on Natalie's shoulder as she lay curled up on the examination table. "Are you going to be all right?"

With tears racing across her face onto the paper sheet, Natalie nodded her head yes, despite knowing it was a lie.

"Is there anyone you would like me to call?"

"No," she forced out. "I'll be fine. I just need to lie here for a minute, if that's okay?"

"It's fine, honey. I need to go check on some other patients. I'll be back shortly," she assured.

Natalie let out a hearty cry as she cradled her stomach. Why did things have to come to this? Fear had urged her to call Aneetra and see if she would meet her here, but no one had answered the phone at her home. Natalie was so scared. She badly wanted to call Troy, however, she knew she couldn't lean on him for support. For the last two weeks, he'd repeated his affirmation to take care of his responsibility, but his unaffectionate behavior and distant conversation overrode any pledge he'd made to her. As much as Natalie needed his comfort right now, she couldn't call him. What happened in this room was only an answer to Troy's coldhearted desires.

Hours later, Natalie was in the comfort of her own apartment, but there was nothing comfortable about how she felt. Tears continued to spill from her eyes as she unsuccessfully tried to erase the memories of what had happened earlier from her mind. It was no use. Her womb was empty and the experience was now branded in her psyche. Her emotions spiraled down a pit of depression, bringing back over eighteen years of suppressed feelings. She had been scarred with deep emotional wounds that had never truly healed. Those scars affected every relationship in her life, including her friendship with Wendy. Perhaps if her heart had not been hardened, Natalie would've been able to connect to Wendy on more than a superficial level. She'd vowed never again to let anyone penetrate the partition around her heart and had done a good job of it…that is, until she'd met Troy.

Why had she allowed herself to fall in love with that man? She should've just stuck with the plan to move back to New York. Children were never a part of that agenda. How could she have been foolish enough to think that she and Troy could live happily ever after? Because of her stupidity, she was now entangled in a web of pain that was so great, she wanted to die. Wounds from her past had been reopened and not even writing her feelings down could help this time. She was very tempted to swallow the entire pile of painkillers that lay on her desk to her right.

Natalie knew she needed to return to her roots and uncover the missing piece to the puzzle of her life if she didn't want to jeopardize her own sanity any longer. She'd make up something and call Alex on the way south. Somehow she had to find a way to move on, but she knew she couldn't continue to bury her past after what had just happened. She had to find answers. Before she began her journey, there was just one more thing she needed to do.

After another long, hard day at work, Troy keyed in the security code to enter his apartment building. The cold March wind followed him into the building. As usual, he checked his mailbox and leafed through the mail on his way up.

Spotting a handwritten envelope with no return address, he assumed it was junk mail and tossed it, along with the rest of the items, on the kitchen counter upon entering his apartment. His message light was blinking and he expected it to be Natalie. They hadn't spoken in three days as she hadn't yet returned any of the messages he'd left on her home, work and cell phones.

"Hey, what's up, playa? I haven't heard from you in a while," called out the voice of his best friend, Elvin Campbell. "Man, did you fall off the face of the earth? I might come that way next weekend with Nicole. Her friend is getting married in Cincinnati and she wants me to ride with her. You know I really ain't tryin' to hang out with a whole bunch of folks I don't know. If you're free, I'll have her drop me off in Columbus and spend the weekend with you. Call and let me know your schedule. Okay? Talk to you later."

Though disappointed it hadn't been Natalie, Troy was glad to hear from Elvin. The two of them had been best friends since third grade, and both had moved from Texas to attend college in Columbus. It had only been two years since Elvin and his family relocated to Chicago. Troy opted to shower before calling Elvin back, walking through his spacious living room—past the black leather furniture, chrome tables and thirty-six-inch flat-screen television to which his Xbox 360 was connected.

As the warm water caressed his body he thought about Natalie and how she was really starting to annoy him. Why hadn't she returned his calls? Yeah, there'd been tension between them lately, but he'd been trying to play it cool despite the fact that she was having this baby without his consent. He'd promised her that he'd take care of his obligations. Why wasn't that good enough? Why had she thought he'd eventually marry her? Marriage was a commitment he would never be ready for.

Troy had been the best man at Elvin's wedding and remembered it as though it was yesterday. Standing at the altar in a rented tuxedo all he could think was *Better you than me...wonder how long this will last.* He had seen marriages fall apart many times before. Everything he'd said to Natalie about police officers and their less-than-successful marriages, he believed was true. He'd witnessed it firsthand through the lives of people on the force. However, his biggest fear was the possibility of continuing the pattern of failed or severely wounded marriages that plagued his family. With the exception of Elvin and Nicole, how could he be successful at something he'd never seen modeled positively?

Truth be told, he was surprised his friend's marriage had lasted as long as it had. He and Elvin had both had dysfunctional home environments growing up. Elvin's father left the family when he was only three. His mother remarried twice to physically abusive men who were not fit to be husbands or fathers. Both sets of Troy's grandparents had marriages rocked by adultery. One of his grandfathers even had four children by a mistress. Though Troy's parents were still married, the marriage had been on and off for as long as Troy could remember—currently off, thanks to his father's most recent affair. Between his mother and his father, Troy had a combination of eleven aunts and uncles—all of them had been divorced at least once.

Perhaps if Troy wasn't so frightened by marriage, Natalie would be the one. Not necessarily because of the baby; he didn't believe that people had to get married just because they had a child together. He figured one error in judgment didn't constitute another. Most people who married just because of a child didn't make it—at least that's how things had worked out for his sister. Troy was very fond of Natalie. He knew that she cared about him and his feelings for her were very intense, but was it love? If it was love, what did it mean?

"Hey, man, what's going on?" Elvin asked when Troy called him back.

"Nothing much…"

"You all right? You sound sad."

"Oh, I'm fine." He hadn't told Elvin much about Natalie and he especially didn't want to mention what was going on now that she had a confirmed pregnancy. He needed time to get his own thoughts together before seeking the advice of anyone else. "I just got off work not too long ago, so I'm a little tired."

"Well, at least it's Friday. You can relax now."

"Not yet…I have to go back in tomorrow."

"I guess somebody has to keep the citizens of Columbus safe, huh?"

"Yeah, something like that. What's been going on with you?"

"The same ol', same ol'—family, church, and work. Life is good, though. I can't complain."

"How are Nikki and the boys?"

"Everyone's doing great. Nikki is still running her catering business from home, and both Joshua and Caleb are playing basketball right now in school. Joshua's a point guard, and Caleb plays center. They're doing pretty good."

The news of the boys playing ball came as no surprise to Troy. It seemed like basketball had been implanted in both his and Elvin's genes. "That's great, man. Tell them both I expect front-row seats when they make it to the NBA."

"They got a long ways to go." Elvin laughed. "Anyhow, so what's up for next weekend? Are you gonna be free?"

"Yeah, come on down. Are the boys coming, too?"

"No, Nik's mom is going to watch them."

"That may be a good idea, I would hate for them to see their daddy get whooped on in Madden," Troy teased, referring to the popular football video game.

"Whatever, man! I see you're still talkin' trash. We'll see how things go when I get down there."

"It'll be good to see you. I'm glad you're coming."

"Yeah, me, too. Listen, man, I'm about to get off this phone. I know you probably want to get some rest before tomorrow. Plus, Nikki and the boys are waiting on me. We're supposed to be going to the movies tonight. I'll give you a call before next weekend."

"Okay. Tell everyone I said hello."

"I will. Talk to you later."

"Cool. Bye." Troy noticed it was almost nine o'clock, and once again he became agitated that he hadn't heard from Natalie. Was she trying to teach him a lesson by avoiding him? He'd catered to her much too often, being the first one to call whenever they'd gotten into it. Not anymore. He didn't know what she was up to, but he wasn't going to let her have the upper hand. He made a pact with himself not to call her the entire weekend. She was obviously being stubborn, and he could play that game, too. He'd wait until she called him. He'd played the waiting game with other women before and experience had taught him that they *always* called first.

Troy got his mail off the counter and sat at the computer

going through it, paying bills on-line. He finally got around to opening the unidentified envelope, expecting it to be a solicitation offer of some kind. It wasn't.

Dear Troy:
I'm writing to say good-bye. There's no need for us to pretend that this relationship is going to work out. We have extremely different ideas about the nature of our relationship and its future. I want one thing, you want another. There's no middle ground. In any event, I want you to know that I enjoyed our time together. You came into my life at a very crucial moment, and being with you really helped me get past some things.

I'm leaving town for a while. I'm at the end of my rope and need to get away. I honestly don't know how long I'm going to be gone. I'll be back in Columbus eventually. Getting away is the best thing for me right now.

If by some small chance you're wondering about the baby…relax, there is no longer a baby. I am no longer pregnant. You should be happy…that's what you wanted, right? If you ever doubt anything about me, never doubt how much I loved you.
Take care,
Nat

…there is no longer a baby…. Troy eyed the statement. What did she mean? Had she gone through with getting an abortion after all? If so, she didn't seem to be taking it well, and Troy couldn't help but feel responsible. Forget about the promise not to call her this weekend. He was too worried to keep it.

Chapter 21

A Cry for Help

Troy entered the apartment by using the spare key Natalie had given him. He stepped in cautiously, flipped on the light and eyed his surroundings. Noticing his habitual actions, Troy had to remind himself that this was not a crime scene. The soft, steady ticking of the wall clock cut through the mysterious silence in the air. Troy circled the living room with his eyes. The once cool, calm and collected police detective was now disturbed, distressed and disenchanted. He was looking for something—anything that would lead him to Natalie's whereabouts.

His feelings about her pregnancy had been pushed aside. Right now, he just wanted to know that she was okay. The words in her letter continued to trouble him. *...there is no longer a baby.... You should be happy...that's what you wanted, right?* True, he'd never wanted the baby, but what price would he pay in the long run for his freedom? He hadn't thought she would take having an abortion this hard. He'd known women who'd done it and they seemed to talk like it was no big deal. Now he felt guilty for pressing the issue. How would he ever forgive himself if she did something to herself because of that?

Not seeing anything significant in the living room, Troy went into Natalie's bedroom and found it in disarray. Several items were thrown across her unmade bed and the floor, while dresser drawers stood open with clothes hanging out of them. Troy stooped slowly and picked up a short-sleeved designer shirt off the floor. He clutched it to his chest. "Where are you, baby?" he softly whispered aloud, wishing that Natalie would jump out of the closet or crawl from under the bed and say that the letter had been a ploy to get him over to her place. As much as Troy yearned to see Natalie, deep down he knew she was gone. From the condition of her room, it was evident that she had left in a hurry. But why?

He wanted to use his connections as a police officer to launch a full missing-person investigation, but legally he couldn't. Natalie had sent him a letter stating that she was leaving of her own free will, and there was no reason to suspect foul play. Confused and emotionally wounded, Troy began to pick up the rest of her clothing, folding it and putting things back in the drawers while racking his brain to find out where she had gone.

He looked at the nightstand where the base of her cordless phone lay. The phone wasn't there, so he pressed the page button on the base and followed the beeping sound into the spare bedroom. Picking the phone up off her desk, he flipped the caller ID, hoping to find a clue.

Troy pressed Talk and hearing a stuttered dial tone confirmed for him that Natalie had at least one unheard message. He pressed the redial button to see who the last person was she had called.

"Hello?" A man answered.

"Hi…um, I'm Detective Troy Evans." Identifying himself this way would give him more credence. "To whom am I speaking?"

"Marcus Bennett. What can I do for you, detective?" The man seemed a little skeptical, but Troy was even more determined to speak with him when he recalled that this man's name had also been on Natalie's caller ID.

"Hi, Mr. Bennett. I'm investigating a possible missing person case—Natalie Coleman. Your number was the last one dialed from her phone and I also noticed several calls placed from your home to hers. What is the nature of your relationship with Ms. Coleman? Are the two of you involved somehow?" He hoped he didn't sound like a jealous lover, but he was. The idea of this dude having phone conversations with *his* girl was disturbing.

"Sir, I don't even know her, but hold on, my wife does. They work together."

A sigh of relief…at least Natalie wasn't cheating on him. Troy held the receiver while Mr. Bennett told his wife to "hurry and get the phone."

"Hello?"

"Is this Mrs. Bennett?"

"Yes, but please call me Aneetra."

"Okay, Aneetra, I'm Detective Troy Evans. Your husband said that you work with a lady named Natalie Coleman?"

"Yes, I do. I've been trying to get a hold of her. Is everything okay?"

"I don't know, ma'am. That's what I'm trying to find out. Your telephone number was the last she dialed."

"Really? When?"

"I'm not sure when, ma'am. You sound surprised."

"I am. I haven't spoken with Natalie all week. If she called my house, she definitely did not leave a message."

"You said you were trying to get hold of her, do you mind my asking why?"

"I wasn't at work on Wednesday and when I went in yesterday, my supervisor told me that Natalie had left her a message saying she had to leave town because of some family emergency. She wanted me to take over some of her projects. I wanted to make sure everything was okay. Something must be wrong if you're calling."

"No, not necessarily. I'm just trying to find out where she could have gone."

"I don't know, sir. She never mentioned anything about leaving to me. The only family I know she has is a grandmother in Mississippi. Maybe she went down there."

"That's a possibility." Troy stated, not truly considering the idea. Natalie had told him that she hadn't been down there since she'd moved to Ohio. He didn't think it would make sense for her to go now under the circumstances. "Do you know anyone else who may have been in contact with her?"

"No, we don't have any mutual friends. But I do know she has a boyfriend. He's a police officer, too. I don't know his last name, and I can't seem to think of his first name offhand."

"Um…that's okay, I'm sure I'll come across him during my investigation…"

"No, give me a second. It'll come to me. His name is Travis…no, Trevor, or Trent—"

"Ma'am, really…you don't have to do this."

"Troy! That's it. His name is Tr—wait a minute… What did you say your name was again?"

Busted!

"You're him, aren't you? You're Natalie's boyfriend?"

"Well…um, yes, I am," he confessed. "Look, I'm sorry I didn't tell you that when I first called. I'm just really worried about her. She wrote me a letter saying she was leaving town, and I don't know where she's gone. I'm trying to do everything I can to find her."

"Well, first thing I suggest you do is be honest with people when you call them."

"I know. Again, I'm sorry. So you don't know where she is?"

"No, I don't. I'm worried about her, though."

"Yeah, I am, too."

"So you're not buying the whole family-emergency story?"

"No."

"Me, neither. Dennison is really picky about people providing documentation for emergency leave. We can take up to two weeks, but you'd better have documentation to back your story or you'll risk losing your job. I would hate to see something like that happen to Natalie. She's been going through so much lately."

"If I give you my cell phone number, will you call me if you hear from her?"

"I—I don't know about that." Aneetra hesitated. "I wouldn't feel right calling you behind her back. If she didn't tell you where she was going then she must not want you to know."

There was something in Aneetra's voice that made Troy wonder if she'd known Natalie had been pregnant, but he didn't call her on it.

"But," Aneetra continued, "I will tell her that you're looking for her. If you happen to speak with her before I do, will you ask her to call me?"

"Yes, I will. I promise," Troy pledged. "I'm gonna let you go. I'm really sorry about calling your house this late."

"Don't worry about it. Your heart seems to be in the right place."

"It is. I just want to find Natalie."

"Try your best to relax. I'm sure she'll contact you eventually."

"I hope so." Frustrated by the lack of information his investigative efforts had yielded, Troy slumped down in the chair at Natalie's desk. He felt solely responsible for her actions. He noticed that a sheet of paper wasn't lying flat on the desk, and he picked it up. It was a poem. The title, "My Secret," drew him into reading its contents:

When I look in the mirror, what do I see? Someone who doesn't like to look back at me.

I close my eyes so very fast; I open them back up and see my past.

If only I could turn back the hands of time, I'd fix all those things that now weigh on my mind.

Taking a trip down memory lane, I see things I did which I now think are insane.

There was a man who had been my first. That experience was by far my worst.

I was so young and very naïve, he planted the seed and I conceived.

What age you ask? I may never reveal; it's between God and me, my lips are sealed.

Now another one is gone, what shall I do? A little voice suggested popping a pill or two.

I must admit that I am very close to riding on the freeway of overdose,

But I got scared and began to cry, I don't know if I am really ready to die.

Tears formed in Troy's eyes. She was obviously hurting. This poem seemed to be a cry for help. He wanted to find her so badly. He wanted to wrap his arms around her and comfort her. He would apologize for being such a jerk when he found out about the pregnancy. If only he knew where to find her….

Troy folded the poem and put it in his back pocket. He

didn't know why he was taking it. Nothing made sense anymore…her letter, his reaction, the poem. He had more questions than he had answers. He pulled out his cell phone and tried to call Natalie on hers. Once again, he got her voice mail. With a trembling voice, he began speaking. "Um…Nat…it's Troy. I really need you to call me. I got your letter today. Please call me. I just want to know you're okay."

Chapter 22

Always Welcome

Natalie lay on her back in the queen-size bed of the small roadside hotel in Tennessee where she'd been secluded. She was now about halfway to Mississippi and planned to get up first thing tomorrow morning to complete the trip. She needed some time to think things through and get over her fears about facing the unknown. She hoped that after all these years her story wasn't still making headlines in the community, but she wondered if the whispers of people who had unfairly labeled her as promiscuous could still be heard.

Her cell phone rang, interrupting her thoughts. Troy's cell phone number flashed across her display screen, so she didn't answer it. A few moments later it beeped, indicating that he had left her a voice message. She listened to it and noted that he'd gotten her letter, but she didn't call him back. She didn't want to talk to him. In fact, she felt stupid for letting her guard down and allowing herself to care about him. She had done a good job of not letting anyone through her defenses until she'd met Troy. Now she was paying dearly for the risk she had taken to love him. Talking to him wouldn't change what had already happened, and he couldn't help her with what she now needed to do.

The next morning, Natalie awoke early to finish her journey. She studied her sad countenance in the mirror as she brushed her hair back into a ponytail. Staring back at her was a woman who had been scarred with deep emotional wounds that had never truly healed. It was as if life had enjoyed mocking her by not allowing her to have a normal childhood. First, she'd been traumatized by the death of her father when she was only five, then she'd witnessed her mother's heartache brought on by her stepfather, Jesse, and to top it all off, when Natalie was thirteen, she had given birth to a child that had been given up for adoption.

Instead of being concerned with normal adolescent issues like acne and peer pressure, her thoughts had been consumed with whether her baby had been a boy or a girl and with dealing with postpartum depression. As if all of that wasn't enough, within weeks of the baby's birth, her mother had ripped her from the only community she'd ever known and the two of them had moved to Ohio. At the time, Natalie had resented leaving Jackson. Now, however, she understood her mother's actions and agreed that getting away was the best thing. Besides Sylvia, no one in Ohio knew the situation, and thus the stigma didn't follow them. What haunted Natalie even more than the circumstances of her pregnancy was that she had given up her baby and had no clue what happened to it. Now she felt as if the only way truly to put the past behind her was to revisit the place where her past began.

* * *

It was sometime mid-Saturday afternoon when Natalie arrived in town. She passed her former elementary school on the way to her grandmother's house and chuckled at the recollection of the time when she was in second grade and got into her first fight. Natalie had been standing in line, waiting her turn to ascend the stairs and go down the slide when a boy named Corey Daniels cut in front of her. When she told him that he needed to go to the back of the line, he responded by saying "yo' mama," and Natalie had hauled off and punched him in the stomach.

Guilt immediately followed the amusement as she continued thinking about the incident. Believing that Corey Daniels had somehow disrespected her mother, Natalie had been quick to defend her honor on the playground. Yet, last year while her mother was in the hospital fighting for her life, she had been busy trying to seduce another woman's husband.

Natalie pulled up across the street from her grandmother's house and she was about to step onto the paved street but decided to wait when she saw a young, slender girl with long copper-brown hair get out of a charcoal, four-door Nissan Altima and go in. Her stomach churned from a combination of nervousness and hunger as she sat back in her car and waited. She assumed the girl would not be there long since there was a female passenger in the front seat. She jumped when her cell phone rang. It was Troy…again. She had originally left her cell phone on in the event her grandmother had tried to reach her, but since she was here now, there was no point in having it on, so she turned it off.

Looking around, Natalie noticed how little the neighborhood had changed. Besides a few updates, the house was just as she remembered it: dark-red brick siding and concrete steps leading to the covered front porch. Down the street was the beauty shop, and across from it the drug store where she and her cousins would buy candy. The memory of her grandmother reaching into her bra and pulling out a rolled wad of cash was still amusing.

Natalie remained in her car for about fifteen minutes before the girl came out and got back in her car. She waited until the car was no longer in sight before stepping out of her own vehicle. The weather in Jackson was much warmer than in Columbus. Her navy-blue cardigan had been all she needed to keep warm the further south she drove. She opened the wire gate in the fence surrounding the property and crept up the stairs. With shaky hands she knocked on the door. "Just a minute," she heard her grandmother call out. Within seconds, the door opened and the big-chested, full-figured, gray-haired woman she called Big Mama stood there.

"Hi…" Natalie said with a faint smile.

"Oh my land!" Big Mama's eyes immediately filled with tears. "Natalie…" she whispered and embraced her tightly.

"I wasn't sure that you'd recognize me…"

"You think 'cuz you're all grown up now, I wouldn't know my own grandbaby?" Ida Mae smiled adoringly.

"I hope you don't mind…I should've called first. My apartment is being fumigated and I thought it'd be nice to come down for a visit…you know…just to say hi…face to face." Natalie was getting teary-eyed herself.

"You know I don't mind. You're always welcome here." She hugged Natalie again. "Where's your stuff? I know you didn't drive down here empty-handed?"

"No, I left everything in the car."

"Go get it and bring it in. I'll go ahead and get some food started."

"Big Mama, that's okay. I can run and get something real quick."

Ida Mae shooed Natalie with her hand. "Nonsense! You ain't gotta go nowhere for nothin'. Just get your stuff, then c'mon in and make yourself at home," she ordered, walking back inside.

Natalie obediently started back to her car to retrieve her luggage as Big Mama's words—*make yourself at home*—sank into her spirit. Though her overall experience in Jackson hadn't been good, Natalie recalled many wonderful memories about being at her grandmother's house. A few tears spilled from her eyes as she thought about how good it felt to be home.

Chapter 23

The God Thing

With her luggage in hand, Natalie stood at the front door for a moment scanning the living room. Though the decor had changed quite a bit, Natalie still felt a sense of familiarity. She hadn't been at this house in years, yet just as she'd expected, the sofa hid under a plastic covering, there was a Bible lying on a tray next to her grandmother's recliner, and Big Mama still had a collage of pictures around the room, though many of the faces in the pictures were new to her.

Spotting a picture of herself in a blue-and-white polka-dot dress on the piano, Natalie set down her bags and walked over to pick it up. In it, her long, dark ponytails hung way over her shoulders, and she had such a bright gap-toothed smile. She couldn't have been more than four at the time because she remembered her father taking her to get ice cream after the photo session, and he had died shortly after her fifth birthday. It touched her heart to see that her grandmother still displayed this picture of her after all these years. Life had been so good back then.

"Natalie?" Big Mama called from the kitchen.

"Yes?" She set down the picture, picked up her luggage and walked toward the sound of her grandmother's voice.

"You can set your stuff upstairs in whatever room you want. My room is still down here," she said and turned toward Natalie. Her hands were covered with flour and there was a pan of grease crackling on the stove.

"Okay," Natalie replied, checking out the kitchen. The light blue wallpaper and the basic, almond-colored appliances were still a little old-fashioned for Natalie's taste, but it was a vast improvement from the yellow-painted walls and puke-green stove and refrigerator that Natalie vividly remembered.

She took her bag and walked up the stairs. Natalie knew exactly which bedroom she wanted. It was the second one to the left—the one she used to stay in as a child.

The wooden door creaked when Natalie pushed it open. She stood still for a moment in astonishment, absorbing the room's appearance. Except for the twin bed in the corner, the room had changed drastically over the years. A light brown carpet now covered the hardwood floor, tan venetian blinds had replaced the white frilly curtains and off-white paint concealed the once-pink walls. No matter how foreign the decor made the room look to her, it was still her room.

It took about twenty minutes for Natalie to unpack all of her things. Afterwards, she rejoined her grandmother in the kitchen. Her mouth watered at the smell of chicken frying. "Do you need any help?"

"No. Everything will be done in a bit. You just sit on down and rest. So, how long did it take you to get here?" Big Mama asked, now chopping lettuce.

"Totally, about twelve hours. I stayed overnight in Tennessee." Really, she had stayed two nights, but admitting it might seem strange and spark further questions.

"How long do you plan on staying?"

"I don't know. Maybe a week or two."

Her grandmother turned and looked at her suspiciously. "It's gonna take them that long to finish your apartment?"

"I don't know. I just thought it would be nice to get away for a while. The fumigation gave me a chance to do so."

"Mm-hmm." There was something about her grandmother's response that suggested she wasn't fully buying her story. "Well, I'm glad to see you."

"I sat out in the car for a while because I noticed you had company and I didn't want to interrupt."

"You must be talkin' about Corrine. She's been down at the center today helping Tommy with the bake sale. That's Toni's daughter."

Toni's real name was actually Antoinette and she was Natalie's father's only sister. "Is Aunt Toni still practicing law?" Natalie asked, recalling how Toni had graduated from law school several years before Natalie and her mother moved to Ohio.

"No, motherhood changed her motives. She said she felt like she was spending too many hours at the office and not enough time at home. She tried teaching for a while, but eventually became a stay-at-home wife and mother."

"Wow…I always thought Aunt Toni would own her own law firm one day. She was so passionate about being an attorney. Every time I see a rerun of *Law and Order*, I think about her. Was the other girl in the car Aunt Toni's daughter, too?"

Big Mama shrugged her shoulders. "I didn't know anyone else was in the car. My guess is that it was probably one of Corrine's friends. She and Toni have been into it because Corrine's been hangin' around with this girl that Toni cain't stand," she chuckled.

"What's so funny about that?"

"Nothin' really. I'm just thinkin' about earlier when I was talkin' to Toni and she was all worked up because Corrine got herself a tattoo. She showed it to me when she was here and my heart 'bout stopped when I saw the word *sexy* written inside a red heart on her shoulder. But, I didn't say anything because Toni had already fussed her out." This time her grandmother laughed heartily. "Turns out that Corrine's tattoo is washable. She scratched it off right in front of me and I got tickled to death. She said she has a whole stack of the same one that she puts on every morning. I told her to let her mama know it was fake so Toni could quit havin' a fit. Toni has her ways at times, especially when she thinks she's right, but she is a really good mother and she loves those children to death."

"How many children does she have?"

"Five altogether—three boys and two girls."

The phone rang, interrupting their conversation. "You want me to get it?" Natalie offered.

"No, I got it, baby. You go on and wash your hands so you can eat."

It was almost one o'clock in the morning—actually two o'clock if Natalie went by Ohio time, but she and her grandmother were still up. After Natalie had eaten, she took a short nap, then she and Big Mama spent the rest of their time talking and looking through old photo albums. "We better get to bed if we're gonna get up for church tomorrow," her grandmother announced.

"Church?"

"Yeah, we got time to get a li'l sleep. Service don't start 'til nine."

"Uh…I didn't really pack anything to wear to church," Natalie commented.

"Chile, ain't nobody runnin' a fashion show. Wear whatever you brought. If you really wanna get somethin' different, we can run up to the shoppin' mart real quick. It's open
twenty-four hours. I got a couple hundred on me right now."
She started to reach into her bra.

"No, that's okay."

"So you just gonna wear whatcha got, then?"

"Well, I…"

"Good, 'cuz when Earl called earlier I'd already told
him that Crystal didn't have to pick me up." She got up
out of her recliner. "Good night, sweetie. I'll see you in
the morning."

Natalie knew she would have a hard time coming up with
an excuse her grandmother wouldn't have a ready response
for, and so she didn't even bother offering a rebuttal,
figuring it wasn't going to kill her to go.

Sunday morning Natalie—in a silver blouse and black
pants—found herself walking into the white-and-gold building alongside her grandmother. Her clothing was definitely
not traditional church attire. From the moment she had
started getting ready, she started feeling self-conscious and
she wished she'd gone out and bought something else to
wear. However, her grandmother reminded her that the
only opinion of importance was God's, and that she need not
overly concern herself with what anyone else would think.
To make Natalie feel more at ease about her apparel, and
to prove her point, her grandmother wore something casual.

Big Mama seemed not to care at all about the disapprov-
ing looks from several people whose expressions said that
surely she knew better than to come to church dressed in a
gray pant suit. Natalie got a kick out of the way her grandmother gracefully pranced to the front row and took her seat,
her demeanor daring anyone to say anything. The only bad

part was that she dragged Natalie up to the front with her and Natalie would have preferred to sit in the back—way back.

Natalie immediately noticed, thankfully, that the wooden pews had been replaced with more comfortable cloth-covered ones and that air conditioning had been installed. People continued piling in until the place was filled to capacity; folding chairs were set along the side walls to accommodate more people. If Natalie didn't know any better, she could've easily mistaken her uncle Earl for her grandfather as he stood in the pulpit adorned in a black robe. Now that the hand-clapping, foot-stomping, singing portion of the service was over, sitting here listening to a sermon was boring with a capital *B!* She tried her best to stay alert, but didn't seem to be successful at it.

Ouch! A painful pinch on her thigh brought her to full consciousness and nearly produced tears. She couldn't believe that her grandmother had done that.

"Wake up… You're too old to be sleepin' in church," her grandmother scolded.

Natalie's leg burned severely and she was a little offended. Last time she'd checked, she was thirty-one years old and could do as she pleased. But, grown or not, she had sense enough to command her eyes to remain open for the re-mainder of the service; she knew Big Mama wouldn't hesitate to give an instant replay.

"May the grace of God rest, rule and abide with you now and forever more…let us all join in together and say…"

"Ahhh-men." Natalie chimed in, relieved the service was over.

Earl and Crystal—who bore a striking resemblance to Sylvia, her sister—stood at the altar greeting people who swarmed to them the second service was over. Natalie would've gone up to speak, but decided to wait until the crowd died down. Instead, she watched patiently as her grandmother spoke to what seemed like every member in the church. Initially, she tagged along behind Ida Mae, but she got tired of smiling at people she barely remembered and took a seat.

"Natalie!" a man ran up and snatched her from the pew to hug her.

"Uncle Tommy?"

"Yeah! It's me!" he gleamed. "I guess you're not used to seeing your unc with a clean shave and a dress suit…"

"You look nice."

"You're so tactful. What you really want to say is that I don't look like a crackhead anymore, right?" he smiled.

Natalie was amused by his humor. "That's not exactly what I wanted to say, but yeah…"

"It's all good. I'm not ashamed of anything God has done for me. So, what brings you all the way here?"

Placing her arms behind her back, Natalie crossed her fingers and said, "I came to visit Big Mama." That wasn't a total lie, but it wasn't the whole truth either.

"How long are you gon' be here?"

"I'm not sure…maybe a week or t—"

"Uncle Tommy, may I use your car tonight?" the girl she had seen at her grandmother's yesterday came up and asked, exchanging a friendly "hello" smile with Natalie. Height was definitely something that ran in their family. The girl was much taller up close than she had appeared to be when Natalie saw her from a distance.

"You had it yesterday…"

"I know," she pleaded, bringing her hands up as though she was saying grace. "*Please*…I promise not to have it back too late."

"Yes, Corrine, you can use it."

"Thank you!" she smiled brightly. "I'll be back. I wanna find Big Mama and say hi."

Tommy rolled his eyes playfully, "Toni and Kenny say I have her spoiled because she'll ask to use my car before she will theirs. Maybe I should start charging her a rental fee. Then she won't want to drive it so much, huh?" he kidded.

Who's Kenny?"

"Toni's husband."

"Speaking of which, where is Aunt Toni?"

"I guess they went out of town last night."

"Too bad. I was hoping to see her and meet the rest of her family."

"Yeah... Well, let me get out of here," he said, rather quickly. "I'll stop by Mama's house sometime this week, and catch you before you leave, I hope." He hugged her again, "It's good to see you, Natalie."

"Thanks. You, too."

When Natalie looked up, Earl and Crystal were walking her way. She spoke with them for a few minutes and was introduced to their daughter. Earl was eager to change out of his robe and said that they'd be by Big Mama's later. When the reunion with her family was over, Natalie resumed her seat on the pew while her grandmother continued socializing.

"I can't get over how different Uncle Tommy looks," Natalie said to her grandmother when they were finally on the way home.

Big Mama smiled. "Ain't it somethin'? Chile, your grand-daddy and I prayed many years, night and day, for that boy. Just when it seemed like our prayers had gone unheard, one Sunday mornin' while Willie James was preachin', Tommy walked in church and gave his life to Christ."

"Really?" Natalie tried to picture the scene in her mind.

"Yep...interrupted your granddaddy's sermon and all. He smelt and looked very bad, but that didn't stop him from comin' up to the altar and cryin' out before God." She stopped to chuckle. "Willie James never did finish his sermon. I doubt he could've said anything that would've moved the congregation the way Tommy's actions did, though. Several people got saved by also givin' their lives to Christ that day."

"Wow…" Natalie said in disbelief as they pulled up in front of the house.

"It was a moment I will never forget. It goes to show that God keeps His word. In Psalm 51:17, the Bible says that He will not despise a broken and contrite heart. Chile, once a person gets saved their whole life changes. What was once a mess turns into a message. Tommy shares his past experiences on drugs to help other young folks. He truly has an inspiring testimony. There ain't one person on this earth that God ain't capable of changin'. All it takes is a willing heart."

Natalie listened to her grandmother, thinking that the God thing might have worked for Tommy, but that's not what she came to Mississippi for. Tommy had had a real bad drug addiction and needed the help of a supreme being to change. Once she found the answers she was looking for, she anticipated being just fine.

Chapter 24

One Sure Thing

Wednesday afternoon Natalie sat at the kitchen table sipping tea and browsing through the latest issue of *Essence* when her grandmother walked into the room.

"I gotta go down to the church for a while. I'd promised to help out with the food pantry today," she announced.

Natalie looked up. "Do you need a ride?"

"No, but thanks anyway. Crystal will be here in a few minutes. I'll probably be there for a couple of hours. Are you gonna be all right by yourself?"

"Yes," Natalie responded, trying to mask how thrilled she was finally to have some time to herself. Since she had arrived in Jackson on Saturday, she'd constantly been in the presence of her grandmother or one of her uncles, and hadn't had time to do what she truly came to Mississippi for.

"You sure you're gonna be all right? There don't be too many young folks there so I didn't think you'd wanna come, but you are welcome."

"No, that's okay. You go ahead. I'll be fine," Natalie insisted.

"Well, if you need me for anything, the number to the church is on the fridge. Sistah Mary Ann Calloway usually answers the phone. I'll tell her to come get me if you call."

"Okay… Oh, do you have a telephone book? I'm almost out of lipstick, and I wanted to call and see if there were any cosmetic places around here that sold MAC."

"What in the world is that?"

"It's a brand name. You know, like Cover Girl or Revlon."

"Chile, I can't keep up with all that stuff." Big Mama laughed. "The phone book is in the living room, underneath the end table right next to my chair."

"Thanks, I'll get it in a bit."

"I'll see you when I get back."

"Okay," Natalie said, bringing the warm teacup to her lips as her grandmother walked away. She stared at the magazine. Her mind was no longer able to process the words printed in the article. When she heard the front door slam, she went into the living room and peeked out the window to ensure her grandmother's departure. As soon as Crystal's red sedan vanished from her sight, Natalie grabbed the telephone book and ran to the kitchen.

As she began flipping through, she was startled when the telephone rang, but she answered it and heard, "Hey, Corrine. Shouldn't you be in class?"

"Huh?"

"Is this Corrine?"

"No, this is Natalie."

"Natalie?" the woman spoke cautiously. "Natalie *Coleman?*"

"Yes, who is this?"

"Oh my God!" she shrieked. "Where's Mama?"

"Aunt Toni?"

"Yes. Now where is Mama?"

"She just left to go to the food pantry or something like

that at the church. You want me to tell her you called when she gets back?"

"No, I'll call down to the church," Toni stated. The next thing Natalie heard was a click.

"Well, hello to you, too," Natalie sarcastically mumbled as the dial tone buzzed in her ear. She turned back to her search of the phone book. She was certain she was doing the right thing. Troy's reaction to her pregnancy and what had happened thereafter had shattered her. She needed to know what had happened to her child. It would be the only way she could bring closure to this open chapter in her life.

Natalie anticipated that the most difficult part about her search would be locating which adoption agency had handled the case. Luckily there weren't tons of agencies to choose from in the phone book. She skimmed through those listed, hoping one of the names would jump out and trigger her memory, but it didn't happen. Thus she ended up dialing the first number she saw.

It was as if the world around her had stopped. Each second seemed like hours. She listened to the sound of her heart thump against her chest as the telephone rang.

"All Care Adoption Services, this is Tammy. How can I help you?"

"Um…" Suddenly her throat was tight. "How do I find a child who was given up for adoption?" she managed to get out.

"Have you filled out a disclosure form?"

"No. What's that?"

"By law, all court records are sealed. However, a disclosure form allows you to voluntarily give out identifying information about yourself. How long has it been since you gave birth to the child that was given up for adoption?"

"It'll be nineteen years in July."

"I can go ahead and send you a form now. Fill it out and file it with the Health Department. That way it'll be on record. However, keep in mind that under Mississippi adoption law, an adoptee can't request identifying information about his or her birth parents until that child turns twenty-one."

"But…I don't understand…"

"If you fill out a form, when your child turns twenty-one, he or she will be able to obtain any identifying information about you listed, such as your name and a contact number. But you won't be able to disclose any information about the birth father. If you want me to, I can send that form out in the mail to you today."

"That's it?" Natalie's distress burst through her speech and tears gushed down her cheeks. "I drove all the way from Ohio for you tell me that I have to fill out a form and then wait at least *two* more years for my baby to look for me? I promise not to disrupt anyone's life. All I want is the assurance that my child has grown up in a loving and healthy home environment," she tearfully pleaded.

"Ma'am, please take a deep breath and try to calm down. I wish I could do more for you…I really do. I—"

Natalie didn't want to hear any consolation speeches. She slammed the phone down so hard she was afraid that she'd broken it. She was able to calm her nerves by convincing herself that All Care Adoption Services was just the first and only place she had called so far. Surely that woman didn't know everything. She would simply call another adoption agency and next time, she'd have better luck.

One by one, Natalie called all of the agencies listed in the Jackson telephone book, receiving similar versions of the process explained by Tammy. Each conversation did its part to extinguish the candle of hope that once had burned within Natalie's heart. She didn't even bother requesting a disclosure form. It didn't guarantee that her child would ever come looking for her.

Her whole life, she'd only be guaranteed one thing: that life would screw her over somehow. So far, that'd been the one sure thing she'd been able to count on.

Natalie pretended to be asleep later when Big Mama came home from church and peeked into her bedroom. She was relieved when she heard her grandmother tiptoe out of the room and shut the door. Natalie lay there staring at the ceiling as tears rolled from her eyes, wondering what in the world she had done to deserve such heartache. It hurt so bad that it was as if she was reliving losing her first child all over again. All she wanted to do was make sure that her baby was okay. Was that really too much to ask?

Ida Mae had barely had the chance to sit down in her recliner when the phone rang. She didn't need caller ID to know who it was on the other end. "Father, please give me the words to say," she prayed before answering.

Chapter 25

Spilled Milk

"Good mornin'," Big Mama said when Natalie walked into the kitchen the next morning. "You came down just in time. I was gonna fix these eggs and then come wake you. I know you gotta be hungry 'cuz you slept like a bear." She poured the eggs into the warm skillet and chuckled. "Were you able to get your Max yesterday?"

"My what?"

"That makeup you were talkin' about."

"You mean MAC?

"MAX, MAC—it all sounds the same to me. Were you able to find it?"

"I changed my mind. I didn't feel like going out."

"Guess who I saw yesterday?"

"I don't know, who?" Natalie mumbled.

"Tawanna Davis, you remember her, don't you?"

"Uh-huh…" Tawanna used to be Natalie's best friend when she was younger.

"She's gettin' married in May. She and her fiancé came by the church to talk to Earl. She don't go there 'cuz she joined her fiancé's church, but Earl is still gonna participate in the ceremony. Lord…time goes by so fast. It seems like just yesterday the two of y'all were sittin' on my front porch playin' with dolls. I tell you, I wish Bessie could see her now." She spoke in a nostalgic tone of voice. Bessie was one of Big Mama's best friends and Tawanna's grandmother. "Anyhow, I told Tawanna you'd be in town for a while. She said she was gonna come by sometime next week and see you."

"Next time you see her tell her that I said hi. I won't be here next week. I'm leaving tomorrow."

"Leavin'?"

"Yes. I should probably get back to Columbus. I plan to say good-bye to everyone today."

"Why are you goin' back so soon? You ain't even been here a week."

"I know it's been a short visit. I just wanted to see how you were doing. I'm anxious to get back to work. I'm hoping to transfer to New York in a few months," she admitted. She was doing what she best knew how to do—stuff her feelings inside and not deal with them at all. It seemed to be the ideal way to move on quickly with her life.

"New York?" Big Mama removed the skillet from the stove. "I ain't heard you say nothin' about goin' there."

"Actually, I was thinking about moving back to New York after Mom died, but—"

"But what?"

"I just delayed my plans, that's all." When her grandmother placed a plate of food in front of her, Natalie said, "I'm really not all that hungry."

"Well, just eat a li'l bit," Big Mama ordered and sat across from her. She hadn't fixed a plate for herself. "After you eat, maybe you'll tell me what's really goin' on."

"What are you talking about?" Natalie protested without touching her plate.

"As glad as I am to see you, I know you didn't come all this way just to say hi, then to wake up this mornin' and say you're leavin' and thinkin' about movin' to New York. Somethin's wrong. You've been here five days and not once have you mentioned New York."

"I haven't mentioned a lot of things to you, but it doesn't mean that I don't think about them."

"Um-hmm…"

"Look, Big Mama, there's a lot going on in my life that you don't know about."

"Like what?"

"Like part of the reason I came down here was to get away from my boyfriend. Things weren't going too well between us. I made up the whole fumigation story," Natalie confessed, avoiding looking her grandmother in the eyes. "But I did want to see you. I could have gone anywhere to get away…I could have even gone to New York, but I came here." There was no need to tell her grandmother about her latest pregnancy or what her true agenda had been. Both were moot issues at this point. What would be the point of crying over spilled milk?

"Boyfriend, huh? I figured you were sweet on someone." She pointed to Natalie's plate. "You better eat that before it gets cold."

Natalie looked at the spread before her. Despite her protest earlier, she was starving. The aroma of the home-made buttermilk biscuits and scrambled eggs made her mouth water. Her roaring stomach convinced her to take a bite. Mmm… "Aren't you gonna eat?"

"Naw, chile, I made this for you. I don't too much eat breakfast even though you cain't tell it by lookin' at me." Her laughter brought a smile to Natalie's face. "So this boyfriend of yours—"

"*Ex*-boyfriend…"

"Okay… Do you wanna talk about what happened with y'all?"

"No, not really. He just wasn't what I thought he was."

"Well, you know that I'm here if you wanna talk…I really hate to see you go so soon."

"I know…I'll be back, I promise."

"I know you have to go back to work, but you've come all this way. Do you think you could at least stay 'til Sunday?"

"Why? What's so special about Sunday?"

"We're havin' a celebration for Tommy in honor of his tenth year bein' drug-free. We usually have a small dinner for him either here or at Earl's. But this year, we're gonna do it at the church immediately after service. Folks from the center will be there."

"You guys really celebrate his recovery on a yearly basis?" Such a celebration seemed unusual to her.

"Like I said, this is the biggest celebration ever, but yeah, we do. What better way to remind ourselves and show others what God can do? I'm sure Tommy would want you to be there. But please don't tell him. It's a surprise. He thinks we're just havin' dinner again. Oh and Tawanna said she was comin'."

"I guess it won't hurt to stay until then. On second thought…I don't know. I don't want to get pinched again. You left a bruise, you know."

Her grandmother smiled. "Soak in some Epsom salts and put a li'l cocoa butter on it. You'll be all right."

Chapter 26

Mumbo Jumbo

Troy was up early Saturday morning after another sleepless night. He immediately looked at his cell phone—still no call from Natalie. It had been a week since he'd received her letter and he wasn't any closer to finding out where she was now than he had been then. He tried calling her again and as he'd expected, her voice mail came on. By now he figured it was pointless to leave yet another message for her since all of his others had gone unanswered. He was relying on Aneetra to keep him informed and the last time he'd spoken with her—yesterday—she hadn't heard from Natalie either—at least that's what she'd told him. Frustrated, Troy got of bed and threw his running gear on. On his way out he left a note on the refrigerator for Elvin, who had arrived in town last night.

The morning air was very breezy, but knowing how cold Ohio winter weather could be, Troy had no complaints. As his size elevens hit the pavement in a rhythmic fashion, he began to warm up quickly. The sounds of passing cars, barking dogs and other morning pedestrians faded as his mind automatically shifted back to Natalie.

The more he thought about his negative reaction to her pregnancy, the angrier he got with himself, and the harder his feet pounded the ground. How could he have been so stupid! After running a couple of miles Troy went back to his residence and found Elvin awake and sitting in the living room, his light skin contrasting drastically with the black sofa. "What's up? Did you get my note?"

"Yeah. I heard you when you left, I just didn't feel like getting out of bed right then and there. I was about to load up Madden…. You wanna get on?"

Troy didn't really feel like playing the Xbox 360, but what else would he and Elvin do this early in the morning? "Let me jump in the shower first."

"Your cell phone was ringing a minute ago."

"Thanks, man." A glimmer of excitement shot through him as he rushed to his bedroom, hoping it was Natalie who had called. "Dang it!" he muttered. It was just a buddy of his from work. Disappointed, Troy ripped off his clothes and jumped in the shower.

The two men had finished playing one game when Elvin suddenly tossed his controller on the table. "Why'd you do that?" Troy asked, still holding his.

"Who is she?"

"Who?"

Elvin shrugged his shoulders. "I don't know. That's what I need you to tell me. I just beat you fifty-nine to six. It's like you weren't even tryin'. Man, I ain't crazy. Something has gotten you all worked up, or shall I say *someone?*" He raised his thick eyebrows and gave Troy a sly smile, pushing his pointy chin further toward the ground.

"I don't know what you're talkin' about. My game is just off, that's all."

"Okay, I'll just play stupid. You know, like I haven't peeped you checking your cell phone every so often like you're trying to make sure it still works. I take it you're expecting a call?"

"Are you a private eye now or something?"

"Oh, so you got jokes, huh? Man, you look as sick as a dog chasing its own tail. You don't have it together, bro?"

Not having the will to continue denying, Troy gave in. "It's that obvious?"

"Yep… Do you want to talk about it? Whoever she is, I have to give her mad props because I never thought I'd see the day when the playa fell in love."

"In love?" Troy frowned as though he was allergic to the word.

"Please don't tell me you're denying that, too."

"I like the girl and all, but no one said anything about being in love."

"Yeah, yeah, yeah… Okay, Sergeant Troy N. D. Nile, what's going on with you and this woman who you like, but are not in love with?"

He pretended not to notice Elvin's sarcasm. "I don't know. It doesn't seem like anything is going on between us. I've been trying to call her since last Friday and I keep getting her voice mail."

"Is she mad at you for some reason?"

"Yeah… I've sort of been a jerk these last few weeks."

"It sounds like you have some serious damage control to do. Why don't you surprise her by sending a dozen roses to her job, or take her out someplace special?"

"I can't…she's gone," Troy said, sadly.

"What do you mean she's gone?"

"She left town. Last week, the same day you called and said

you were coming here, I got a letter from her saying that she had left. I've tried calling her at least a hundred times."

"Something else must have happened to make her leave town besides something you said. Did you cheat on her?"

"No."

"Did you hit her?" Elvin asked, giving Troy a sideways glance of disapproval.

"No! I would never lay a hand on her."

"Well, what happened? It doesn't make sense for her to leave town just because y'all got into it."

"She was pregnant." Troy confessed.

"Pregnant?"

"Yes. And I forced her into having an abortion." Troy was ashamed and couldn't look his friend in the eyes. "She wanted to keep the baby and possibly get married. I told her I didn't want to do either, and now she's gone." He cleared his throat to mask his quivering voice. "I miss her, man…I really do."

"In all the years we've known each other I've never seen you this distraught over a female. You're in love with her."

"I really don't want to be." Troy didn't deny the accusation this time. "Love is such a tricky word. Why can't two people get along, have a good time and just be happy? Why does everything have to center around the L-word? Natalie and I would be kickin' it like we've always done if she just hadn't gotten pregnant."

"Man, you've been my boy for a long, long time. I have to be real with you. You can't keep being scared of long-term, intimate commitments."

"Scared? You've been my best friend since grade school. Call me crazy, but that sounds like a long-term commitment to me."

"You're right, it is. But that still doesn't mean that you're not afraid of letting a woman get close enough to your heart that you'd marry her."

"Getting married and starting a family might work for you, but everyone doesn't have those goals. Who said I wanted the wife, white picket fence, two-point-five kids and the little dog? Besides, that picture only lasts for a while. Afterwards, she'll have the house, the kids and the dog, and I'll be left paying child support and alimony for the rest of my life."

"See! Why'd you have to put the latter part on it? Why couldn't you end with the description of a happily married family with children?"

"Because that's not reality. Reality is that most marriages will end in divorce."

"It's sad, but nowadays that is true. Don't think that Nicole and I haven't had hard times in our marriage. The difference is that we have both committed to working this thing out for life, the way God intended it to be."

"And what makes you think God intended it to be forever?" Troy challenged. He believed in God, but not to the extent that Elvin did. Elvin was on some type of religious trip—going to church all the time and reading the Bible like he didn't have a regular life. Troy wasn't on all of that. He considered himself to be a good person. He didn't do anything immoral and tried his best to maintain his integrity. That was really all it took to get to Heaven.

"Marriage is a covenant between a man and a woman, honored by God. It was first instituted with Adam and Eve. In Mark 10:9, Jesus says that what God has joined together, let no human tear apart. Technically, that means the marriage should only end when one of the spouses die."

Troy rolled his eyes. "Please don't start with the Bible study."

"You asked."

"Yeah…well, I'm sorry I did."

"Look, I'm definitely not trying to preach to you. This is something you'll have to work out on your own. Remember, your marriage will be what you make it. It doesn't have to be like your parents', your grandparents' or that of any of your other relatives. Be determined that if you get married, your marriage will last. That's what I did."

"Well, good for you."

"Get mad at me if you want, but you know I'm gonna always tell you the truth."

"No, what you're really saying is that I need to join a church so that I can have the relationship with God that you have, and everything will be peachy-keen in my life. I can get married to Natalie and the two of us can live out the fairytale, happily-ever-after life."

"I have never said that."

"Then what are you saying?"

"First of all, let me clarify one thing—there is a big difference between joining a church and having a relationship with God. In order to have a relationship with Him, you must confess Jesus Christ as your Lord and Savior and believe that He died for your sins and rose again…that's what it means to be saved. Saved people should want to join a church so they can learn more about God and fellowship with other believers. Unfortunately, many people substitute joining a church for salvation, but it truly can't be done."

"Well, whatever…"

"As far as having a peachy-keen life goes—it's not so. It will never be so. Salvation is the assurance that when a person dies his or her soul will reside in Heaven for the rest of eternity. It allows one to tap into God's resources of maintaining such things as joy in spite of sorrow and peace in the midst of turmoil. If you don't remember anything else from the Bible, remember Matthew 6:33, which says 'Seek first the Kingdom of God and His righteousness; and all these things will be added unto you.' You're never really going to have peace and be able to get over your fears until you're willing to put your life and everything that's happened in it into God's hands."

"Enough already with the Bible study. I get your point!" Troy was getting irritated. None of that mumbo jumbo would do him any good with finding Natalie. She was his major concern right now. "Why didn't I think of that before?"

"Think of what?"

"I know someone who can help me find Natalie."

"Cool. I hope it works out."

"I do, too.... Look, man, I didn't mean to snap at you. I know you were just trying to help me. Believe it or not, I heard everything you said. I guess it's just gonna take some time for me to work all of this out."

Elvin nodded in agreement.

"Now, so we don't sit here and talk about my woman troubles all day, let's go get something to eat. I'm starting to get hungry."

"Cool, but let's play one more game of Madden first. Now that you've cleared your mind, I want to make sure I beat you fair and square. I don't want you crying mental distress when I put another whuppin' on you."

"You better hang on to the previous win because it'll be your only one from here on out. I'm about to put it on you for real this time. I see you got a little arrogant because I let you win."

"Oh, bring it on, partnah!"

"Yeah, you might know a li'l somethin' about the Bible, but I got a patent on Madden...I even got a scripture. 'Seek first Troy Evans and his wisdom and all the knowledge of football will be added unto you.'" Troy smiled, plopping the other controller in Elvin's lap.

Elvin could do nothing but laugh. "It's good to see you acting like yourself again."

Chapter 27

True Deliverance

Once again Natalie sat in the front pew with her grandmother as service began, this time hoping that seven hours of sleep last night and the Red Bull she'd drunk on the way over would guarantee her attentiveness. Some good the Epsom salts and cocoa butter had done...evidence of her grandmother's assault had yet to fade completely.

"The Bible tells us that there was a woman who suffered for twelve years with an issue of blood," Earl said, using Mark 5:25-34 for his text. "Picture, if you will, what it's like dealing with the same problem for that long. Some of us catch a two-day headache and we're ready to die," he chuckled lightly. "Can you imagine what it would be like if any kind of ailment afflicted your body for twelve years? Scripture tells us that this woman had sought physician after physician, hoping to find a cure for her condition. After exhausting all of her resources, she was no better. As a matter of fact, her condition was worse."

"Imagine the level of faith it took for her to believe that just by touching the bottom of Jesus' garment, she could be healed of her disease. That's what I call being desperate for deliverance. Desperate people are those who have become frustrated by trying one solution after another. They lay aside their pride and are willing to try anything because they believe that something has to work."

Natalie wasn't sure if it was genuine interest or fear of another ambush, but to her surprise, she was actually being drawn into the sermon.

"The Galilean woman suffered from a blood disease, but there are many people sitting in this congregation today who also suffer from an affliction. Your disease is one that has plagued all of mankind. It's called sin and is what separates us from God."

"John 3:16 says that 'God so loved the world, He gave His only begotten Son that whoever believes in Him should not perish, but have everlasting life.' Jesus is the means by which we can be forgiven for our sins and be connected with God…. Do me a favor, will you?" Earl addressed the entire congregation. "Turn to John 3:16 in your Bibles and repeat that scripture to yourselves, but substitute the word *world* with the word *me*."

Big Mama opened her Bible to the aforementioned passage and handed it to Natalie who began following her uncle's instructions. "For God so loved *me* that He gave His only begotten Son that whosoever believeth in Him should not perish, but have everlasting life." She'd learned that scripture long ago as a child in Sunday-school class, but there was something about substituting the word *world* with *me* that personalized it in a way that she'd never felt before, and the phrase cycled through her mind.

Earl signaled for the congregation to stand up. "If you have not yet accepted Jesus Christ as your Lord and Savior, why don't you do so now? Don't you want deliverance from your disease of sin? Sin can manifest itself in a variety of ways—alcoholism, drug abuse, sex and depression among other things. Maybe you've tried remedies like self-help books, pursuit of money or even impure relationships. Know that these things may provide temporary relief, if any at all, but there is only one solution as true deliverance can only come from Jesus."

Natalie continued repeating, "For God so loved *me*," under her breath.

"Jesus wants to save you and no matter what you've done, there's nothing in this world that God is not able and willing to forgive you for. First John 1:9 says that 'He is faithful and just to forgive you of your sins.' If you don't have the assurance that you would go to Heaven if you died tonight, then you need Jesus in your life. Won't you step forth?"

Natalie felt a tug at her heart, prompting her to go, but her feet stayed planted. She was scared. Committing her life to Jesus would be a big step. Could she really do something like that? Tears mixed with mascara ran down the sides of her face. Her eyes met Earl's directly and as much as she wanted to break his gaze, she couldn't.

"I sense there may be someone here who desires salvation, but you're afraid. Trust me when I say you have absolutely nothing to lose, but everything to gain," he spoke softly, still looking at Natalie. "Remember that God knows the secrets of every sinner. He knows the things that haunt us—the things we can't seem to get past. You've tried everything else, why not try Jesus?"

Natalie's legs trembled. She'd allowed the painful experience from her childhood to harden her. She'd searched for peace through the means of modeling, money and men, but none had given it to her. The depths of her soul cried out for more and she wailed from the pit of her stomach as she slowly took steps toward the altar and dropped to her knees.

She didn't understand how God could love her or why He would even want to after the mess she'd made of her life. But the fact that He did love her despite all brought her emotions pouring out from within.

"Asking Jesus into your life is one of the best decisions you can make." Earl stated after those responding to the altar call came forth. "I'm gonna lead you in a prayer. I promise that if you say this prayer and mean it with all of your heart, you will be saved. But there is a catch," he warned. "You must truly repent in your heart. This means that you must be *so* sorry for your sins that from this day forward, you're willing to change your course of action. Anyone can come up front and say what I tell them to say, but if there isn't true repentance behind the words, then that's all they are—words. If you are honestly ready for a difference in your life then I want you to repeat the following prayer after me: Heavenly Father…"

With her eyes closed and still bent over at the altar, Natalie asked Jesus to forgive her for all her sins and to come into her heart.

Natalie was congratulated by her grandmother, uncles and several others after the service. She and the others who had given their lives to Christ received a daily devotional guide and a study Bible with both the King James and the New International versions. Before they all headed to the basement where Tommy's celebration would take place, Crystal promised to have Earl put together a list of recommended churches in Columbus so Natalie would have somewhere to go when she returned home.

Natalie enjoyed seeing how excited people were as they commemorated Tommy's redemption from drugs. There were balloons, confetti and banners all over the place, as if it was a graduation party or something. Seeing Antoinette seated at a table talking with a man, Natalie went up to her. "Hey, Aunt Toni."

"Um…hi, Natalie," her aunt responded with what seemed to be a forced smile.

After so many years of not seeing one another, Natalie figured that their reunion was at least worthy of a hug, but all she was able to get from her aunt was a simple and dry "hi." She wondered what in the world was up with her aunt's attitude.

"Hello," the gentleman spoke. His thick mustache spread evenly across his upper lip.

"This is my husband, Kenny." Toni announced. "Kenny, this is Natalie—the daughter of my brother, James, who died years ago."

"Oh," he said softly, quickly looking away then grabbing both his and Toni's cups. "I'm gonna throw these away and find Brother John. I've been meaning to talk to him about something. It was nice meeting you," he said to Natalie before hurrying away.

"I'm sorry, did I interrupt something?"

"No, not at all." The words from Toni's mouth did not match the cold expression on her dark-brown oval face.

Natalie sat in Kenny's empty chair. "I just wanted to say hi. I haven't seen you since I've been here."

"Yeah…. speaking of which, how long do you plan on staying?" Toni stared in Natalie's direction, looking past her instead of directly at her, which added to Natalie's feelings of discomfort.

"Probably just another day or two…"

"What brought you all this way?"

"I had some stuff going on—I just needed to get away for a li'l while." Toni didn't say anything and there was an awkward silence. "So…I hear you have a family now," Natalie still sought to break the ice.

"Yeah, I do—three boys and two girls."

"I saw one of your daughters last Sunday—Corrine, maybe?"

Toni's jaw tensed. "Yes."

"She's very pretty. What grade is she in?"

"Thanks. She's a freshman in college."

"Really?" Natalie was surprised. "It doesn't seem like you'd have a child that old."

"Yeah, well Kenny wasn't child-free when we married, you know?"

"No, I wouldn't know. I just met him, remember?"

"Listen, I need to go find my husband. It was good seeing you, Natalie. I hope you have a speedy and safe trip home." Toni got up and left.

Natalie continued sitting at the table, trying to make sense of the encounter with her aunt. Toni had always been very loving and generous toward her. Natalie remembered the Barbie dolls she'd get as presents from her aunt "just because," or how Toni would occasionally take her and her cousins out to a movie. Though she and Toni didn't get to spend loads of time together, it was enough time that Natalie was bothered by her aunt's current behavior; she didn't understand why Toni seemed so abrasive. Natalie wondered if perhaps Toni was upset about their phone conversation last Wednesday. Although Natalie didn't think she had said anything out of the way that day, in retrospect, she wondered if maybe she had.

"Natalie!"

Hearing someone shout her name, Natalie turned and almost fell out of the chair when she saw Tawanna. She stood up to embrace her.

"Wow! It's so good to see you," Tawanna said with a smile that lit up her smooth, mocha-brown face. "You look so pretty."

"Thanks, you, too." She meant it. Tawanna's tall slim figure looked as if it was in perfect shape underneath her tan, short-sleeved, knee-length dress. Natalie stared at her friend in awe. The once scrawny girl with braces and acne had grown up to be an extremely gorgeous woman and would definitely be fierce competition for Natalie if the two of them were ever on a runway together.

"So how long are you here for?" Tawanna asked, swooping one of her long black spiral curls out of her face. Natalie couldn't help but notice the large diamond rock resting on her hand.

"Not too long. I would've been gone a couple of days ago, but I stayed for this party. I'm glad I did, too. It's nice."

"Yeah, it is. Tommy has come a long way."

"I hear congratulations are in order. My grandmother told me you're getting married in May."

"Yes…I am," Tawanna beamed, quickly looking down at her engagement ring with admiration. "If Andre were here, I'd introduce you to him, but he couldn't make it. I should really be the one congratulating you. I saw you go up to the altar. I'm happy for you. It's a big step committing your life to Christ, but you made the right decision."

"Thank you. I know. I'm a little nervous though. I'm not sure if I can really do this whole Christian thing," Natalie admitted.

"Girl, none of us can do it on our own. That's why God's Holy Spirit will guide you every step of the way. Just take it one day at a time. You'll be all right."

"I hope so…"

"You will, trust me," Tawanna reassured. "Natalie, it's so good to see you. I wish I could stay and chat for a while, but I have to get out of here. I have a meeting with my matron of honor. Will you be in town on Friday? I'm having a bridal shower that night and would love for you to be there."

"We'll see…that might be a possibility."

* * *

"Should I have waited until I understand the Bible more to get saved?" Natalie asked her grandmother later that evening.

"Chile, I've been saved for over fifty years and I still don't know everything."

"You could have fooled me."

"I know a lot, but I *learned* a lot. When I first got saved, I didn't know much either. Probably about as much as you, if not less. Like babies in the real world learn things as they grow, you will, too. You're a newborn Christian right now. The more you really seek to understand God's word, the more you will."

"Big Mama, I have done some really shady things in my past. Do you think people will really believe that I'm saved?"

"Folks will always try and find a reason or two to put you in hell. Don't even waste your time tryin' to convince them of your salvation. You just hold your head up and keep your focus on Jesus. Don't let nobody fool you. We all had some things that God delivered us from. Ain't nobody came to Jesus with wings under their arms. We all got skeletons, honey, including me."

Natalie laughed nervously. "I'm having a hard time believing that one."

"Chile, I got a whole graveyard to myself in Mississippi!"

Chapter 28

Act of Nature

Natalie lay in bed the next morning going over the previous day's events. Who would've thought that she, of all people, would be a Christian after the numerous sins she had committed over the years? But, she knew it was true. The moment she repented and asked God for His forgiveness, He gave it. It was amazing how much of a difference one single day had made in terms of her emotional stability. Though it still hurt her a great deal that she couldn't find her child, Natalie trusted that with Jesus in her life, the wounds would eventually heal. There was still a lingering question in her mind about whether she should move back to New York. She thought she'd had her mind made up, but now she wasn't so sure. Rather than focusing on a modeling career, she really wanted to concentrate on her new life and grow closer with God, which is why she eagerly cracked open her new Bible and read 2 Corinthian 5:17, which she and her grandmother had also gone over last night.

"Come in," she said when her grandmother gently tapped on the bedroom door.

"Did I wake you?" Big Mama walked in with the cordless phone in her hand.

"No, I wasn't sleep. I was actually reading my Bible." Natalie said, proudly observing her grandmother's approving smile.

"Sylvia's on the phone. She wants to talk to you, if that's okay."

"Sure." Natalie sat up in bed, wondering what in the world Sylvia could want.

"If you're hungry, I got some cheese grits ready downstairs," Big Mama said before walking out of the room and shutting the door.

"Hello."

"Natalie," Sylvia sounded a littlie nervous. "I'm sorry to bother you, but Richard is on the other line. He wants to tell you something."

"Okay," Natalie spoke cautiously. "What's going on?"

"Troy came by my office this morning," Richard announced.

"I'm sorry, did you say *Troy* came by?"

"Yeah, he was actually waiting for me when I showed up to work."

"What did he say?"

"He tried not to say too much, but he did tell me that you all had been seeing each other since the day I introduced you. It was obvious that the two of you had had a falling out of some kind. He was wondering if I knew where you were. I didn't tell him I did. I just said that I'd let you know he was concerned if I spoke with you. I'm not trying to get in the middle, but the guy looked worried sick. If it's okay with you, I at least would like to let him know you're okay. I promise not to tell him where you're at."

"No, Richard. That's okay. I'll call him myself."

"Are you sure? I don't mind calling him if you don't want to."

"Yeah, I'm sure."

"Okay. Well, I won't hold you. I'm due in court pretty soon. I hope you have a safe trip back."

"Thanks, I will."

"I'll talk to you later, Sylvia," Richard said before hanging up the phone.

Natalie heard a click, but she wasn't sure if Sylvia had hung up also. "Hello?"

"I'm still here."

"I'm gonna get off the phone and call Troy."

"Oh, okay. I have some things I need to do before I start class anyhow. Tell Ida Mae that I said goodbye."

Natalie reached inside her purse for her cell phone which had been off since she'd arrived in Mississippi. She turned it on and listened to several heartfelt pleas from Troy. She didn't really know what to say. She'd never expected him to take her leaving town so seriously. She honestly hadn't thought he would care so much.

"Natalie!" Troy exclaimed, sounding as if his entire face had lit up. "Oh my God, baby, where are you? I've tried calling you a hundred times."

"I know. My cell phone has been off. I just got your messages. I'm at my grandmother's."

"Your grandmother's…in Mississippi?"

"Yes."

Troy sighed. "I'm glad to know that you're all right. After I got your letter and then I read the poem, I was so worried about you."

"What poem?"

Troy was silent.

"What poem?" Natalie asked more assertively.

"I'm sorry, okay? I should never have read it. I was so

worried about you after I got the letter, I went over to your apartment hoping that you would still be there and I saw the poem on your desk."

"You went through my stuff! How could you violate my privacy like that?"

"I wasn't trying to…I just happened to see it lying there."

Natalie was both embarrassed and angry. That poem contained intimate feelings that she hadn't intended to share with anyone. "I can't believe you read it!"

"Baby, I'm sorry. I know it was personal…something that I never should have done. But before you go off on me, hear me out, will you?"

"I'm listening…" Natalie said, halfheartedly.

Troy took a deep breath. "There's no easy way for me to say this…I've been a jerk lately. It's not because of anything you did or didn't do. It's me. I've been a complete fool. Remember the night you asked me if I loved you?"

"Yes."

"I do."

"Troy, there's no need to say all of this because you feel guilty."

"I don't feel guilty—well I do, but that's not why I'm telling you this. I'm trying to express myself to you. I love you, Natalie. I just don't want to get hurt. I've seen people in love so many times get their feelings trampled on, and I don't want to be one of them."

"Don't you think I was scared of getting hurt, too?"

"I'm sure you were, baby, and I'm sorry for hurting you. I said some cruel things and I can't take them back, but I really want you to understand where I was coming from. I have a messed-up family history. When you mentioned that you were pregnant and us possibly getting married, I freaked. There is not one example of a successful marriage in my family. It's like some kind of curse, and I'm scared I won't be a good father or husband because I've never seen those roles modeled to me. That's why I wanted you to have an abortion."

"It's easy to say all of this now that I'm not pregnant anymore," she said, not sure if she should allow herself to believe Troy's explanation, although she could under-stand it. She knew firsthand how a person could be impacted by the past.

"No, it's not easy at all." Troy adamantly rejected. "This is hard! You're the first woman I've ever attempted to explain myself to. I wouldn't be doing so if I didn't love you. My hands are shaking because I'm scared to death that I've lost you. All because I foolishly pressured you into getting an abortion. I—"

"I didn't get an abortion."

"You didn't?"

"No. I considered it, but then I made up my mind that I wasn't going to let my happiness about the baby be depen-dent on yours. I'd planned to have the baby with or without your support."

"But the letter said that you're not pregnant? Did you just say that so I'd leave you alone? Are we still having a baby?"

Natalie was pleased to hear Troy use the plural pronoun *we* instead of asking if *she* was having the baby. Sadly, she couldn't tell him yes. "No…I had a miscarriage. I didn't bother going into detail when I wrote the letter because I didn't think it was important to you. I figured you'd just be relieved to know I wasn't pregnant anymore."

"Oh, baby, I'm so sorry. I had no idea. Are you okay now?"

Natalie heard the authenticity in Troy's voice, and tears welled up in her eyes. "Yeah, I guess. There's really nothing I can do about it. The doctor said I didn't do anything wrong. My fetus just didn't have all the necessary elements it needed to develop. It was an act of nature," she replied solemnly, not wanting to dwell on that awful experience.

"Can I ask you a personal question without upsetting you further?" Troy seemed hesitant.

"Go ahead…"

"How long has it been since your last miscarriage?"

"Huh?"

"You wrote in your poem 'now another one is gone.' When I first read it, I assumed that you were talking about a previous abortion. But in light of what you just told me, I see you were talking about a miscarriage. "

"I really don't feel like talking about that right now."

"Okay. I'm sorry for prying. So…when are you coming home? You are coming back, aren't you?"

"Yes, of course. I was planning to leave this morning, now I'm going to stay another week. I ran into an old friend of mine yesterday who invited me to her bridal shower this Friday. I want to stay for that, go to church with my grandmother on Sunday, and then leave next Monday morning."

"Promise you'll call me when you get back."

"I will."

"Oh, by the way, you might want to call Aneetra. She was worried about you, too."

"How do you know that?"

"Well…when I was at your apartment, I sort of pressed the redial button to see who the last person was you had called, and I ended up calling her house."

"You're a real Inspector Gadget, aren't you?"

"Sorry…I just wanted to find you. Aneetra mentioned you might be in Mississippi, but I didn't think it was plausible at the time. Did you tell your grandmother about the baby?"

"No. Believe it or not, I told her my apartment was being fumigated."

Troy laughed. "Was that the best you could do?"

"At the time. I don't think she believed me anyhow. She knows the truth now—well not about the baby, but she knows I came down here to get away for a while."

"I hope you're having a nice time. Baby, I hate to get off the phone, but I have to. Please call me the minute you get back because I really want to see you."

"I will."

"Okay, I'll talk to you later."

"All right, goodbye." Natalie held the phone in her hand for a few minutes, trying to make sense of everything that had taken place. Was Troy pulling her leg or did he sincerely have feelings for her? She didn't know what to think. She wasn't going to get her hopes up only to be let down again.

"Hey, it's Natalie," she said when she called Dennison.

"Oh my goodness, girl! Where are you?" Aneetra lowered her voice as though she wanted to keep anyone else from overhearing her conversation.

"I'm in Mississippi."

"I thought you might be going there. I have a friend who works in personnel and I asked her to check your file to see if your grandmother's name and number were listed as an emergency contact."

"It's not."

"I kind of figured that out already," Aneetra kidded. "Have you spoken with Troy?"

"Yes, and he told me that he called you one night."

"One night? Girl, that man has been calling me like a bill collector. So, is everything all right? You had me pretty worried."

"Yeah, I just needed to get out of town. I lost the baby…" she revealed.

"What! Oh, Natalie, I'm so sorry to hear that. Are you okay?"

"I'm fine. It was hard at first, but I'm dealing with things slowly. So what's been going on at the office?"

"The same ol' stuff."

"I know I'll have a ton of work to catch up on when I come back."

"Don't worry, you won't. I got your back. Have you spoken with Alex at all?"

"No. I left her a message saying I would be gone for a while. Why?"

"Just wondering. In your message, did you say anything about losing the baby?"

"No."

"How long do you plan on staying in Mississippi?"

"I was going to stay until the end of the week, but maybe I should leave today so I can come back to work tomorrow. Your bringing up Alex makes me think my job may be in jeopardy."

"I'm sorry. I don't mean to frighten you. Initially I was concerned about you losing your job, but I didn't know about the miscarriage then. Don't worry, anything medical-related does qualify as emergency leave. You traveled all that way, no need to rush back now. If you want, I'll mention to Alex that we've spoken. I'll just tell her that you're having some personal issues and needed to get away. You can fill her in on whatever details you wish when you return."

"Sure, if you don't mind…"

"Naw, I don't mind at all. She's not in today, but I'll talk to her when she comes in tomorrow. You know she likes me, so I'm sure whatever I say to her will carry a lot of weight."

"Thanks, Aneetra."

"No problem. That's what friends are for."

The word *friend* made Natalie smile. Aneetra's perseverance to get to know Natalie had paid off. With her kind and consistent efforts, she'd managed to penetrate Natalie's heart to the point where Natalie felt proud and extremely blessed to have her as a friend. "Guess what?"

"What?"

"I got saved yesterday!"

"Are you serious?"

"Um-hmm."

"Oh my goodness!" Aneetra wailed. "That is so awesome! I can't begin to tell you how excited I am to hear that."

"I knew you would be," she said just as her grandmother knocked on the door. "Come in."

"I'm sorry, I didn't know you were still on the phone," Big Mama whispered and started to back out of the room.

"No, stay. I'm about to get off. Aneetra, I'll give you a call later, okay?"

"That's cool. I need to get back to work anyhow."

"Have a good one."

"Girl, you don't have to worry about that. You've just made my day with your good news."

Natalie laughed as she hung up the phone.

"Is everything okay?" Her grandmother took a seat next to her on the bed.

"Yes. That was a friend of mine from work. Sylvia and Richard called to tell me that Troy had been asking about me."

"Who's Troy?"

"My boyfriend…"

"Boyfriend, eh? I thought he was your *ex*-boyfriend…"

"You know what I mean…" Natalie blushed.

"This fellah must be pretty worried about you. Are you gonna let him know you're okay?"

"I've talked to him already. I'm still not sure about what to think about everything, though. He did open up to me a lot. I guess that does mean something."

"Is he saved?"

"No, I don't think so. At least he's never said anything about it."

"I suggest you take some time and not try and rush this relationship. You just got saved yesterday and the devil would love to divert your attention away from Jesus and onto Troy. Start prayin' for the young man. If he's the one, God will eventually get his attention. You and Troy will be less likely to have such major fallouts if both of you are applying God's word to your lives."

"Yeah, I guess…I'm not sure if I'm willing to allow myself to get hurt by him again."

"Remember that no one's perfect. People are gonna disappoint you in life whether they are saved or not. We're human so we're gonna make mistakes. The important thing is that by trustin' God, we put our faith in Him and not people."

"I know…. You don't have to worry about me, Big Mama. I'm definitely being careful this time around." Natalie leaned her head on her grandmother's shoulder just as a growl came from her stomach. Both she and Big Mama laughed. "Are the cheese grits still hot?"

"I don't know about hot, but they are warm."

"Good enough…" Natalie gave her grandmother a hug. "Thanks."

"For what?"

"Just for everything. I love you," she said, the initiator for the first time, making a conscious choice no longer to hold her feelings captive. In this case, love was definitely worth the risk, especially where her grandmother was concerned.

"I know you do, baby, and I love you, too."

Chapter 29

It's a Deal

"Natalie!" Tawanna exclaimed and wrapped her long, slender arms around her tightly. "I'm so glad you came."

"Thanks for asking me to come."

"Y'all ready to get started?" one of the hostesses yelled—her question really was meant as a directive.

Tawanna gently held Natalie's arm and escorted her to a seat so the two of them could sit together. As an icebreaker, each person was asked to stand up, introduce herself and state how she knew Tawanna. When Natalie's turn came she said, "I've known Tawanna probably my whole life. Our grandmothers were really good friends and we did a lot of stuff together." Her speech was probably the shortest of all, but that was fine with her. Natalie recognized a few familiar names from back in the day, but for the most part, she was a stranger as no one gave any sign that they recognized her.

They played several games; Natalie had so much fun she

rolled with laughter as she and her teammates vied against the other women. She was glad she had come.

"So, when are you going back to Ohio?" Tawanna asked later, while waiting for her guests to finish eating so she could open her presents.

"Monday morning. I want to go to church with Big Mama one more time."

"Miss Ida Mae will like that. I may not get to see you again before you leave. I promised a friend I would help her move this weekend. We have each other's information, though. I'd definitely love for us to keep in tou—"

"Well, cuzzie, I gotta admit, your shower is pretty live considerin' the fact that there ain't no naked men." A woman came up and loudly interrupted their conversation. Her short, blond, boyish haircut did not complement her dark, full face.

"I told you that this wasn't gonna be that type of party. Natalie, do you remember my cousin, Kya? She used to babysit us sometimes at my grandmama's, although most times we pretty much watched ourselves." She laughed.

"Yes, I do." Kya was about six years older than Natalie and Tawanna. The times when Kya had kept the girls, she had sent them upstairs or outside to play while she and her friends did their own thing.

"Oh snap…you're *that* Natalie?" Kya's voice elevated. "I heard you say somethin' about your grandmama earlier. You're Miss Ida Mae's granddaughter."

"Yep."

"I remember you. Where you been hiding out at?" She was so loud that she drew the attention of several others to their conversation.

"In just a few minutes Tawanna will open her presents," Monique, one of the bridesmaids, shouted.

"I live in Columbus, Ohio, now."

"That's *right*...you moved up there after you had a baby, right?"

Natalie felt the blood rush to her cheeks. She'd been managing to deal with not finding answers to what had happened to her child, but she'd never expected anyone to throw the situation back up in her face.

"Kya, I'm sure Natalie isn't up for an interrogation right now." Tawanna jumped in.

"Ain't nobody tryin' to intergate...intragi...whatever you said...I ain't tryin' to do that. I was just makin' small talk."

"Well, now is not the time for that," Tawanna stressed.

"Then let her tell me that. She's grown and can speak for herself."

Natalie looked on as Kya and Tawanna went back and forth. She wanted to tell Kya to mind her own blankety-blank business, but the words jammed in her throat.

"Anyhow, as I was sayin' before I was so *rudely* interrupted...I remember you now. You look good for havin' a baby. Maybe because you were so young, huh? Yeah, Ms. Ida Mae and my grandmama thought I was the fast one between us three, but you proved them wrong." Kya laughed loudly.

The louder Kya was, the quieter everybody else at the shower got. Natalie could feel at least a dozen pair of eyes gawking at her. Kya had viciously resurrected her pain. Her heart burned within her chest and her esophagus felt as though it was tied in knots. The hostess of the bridal shower was slowly setting the gifts in front of Tawanna, obviously digesting Kya's words.

"Chill out, Kya," Tawanna ordered firmly through gritted teeth and a forced smile.

"I couldn't resist," Kya said after she'd finished laughing. "You ain't gotta be so uptight, Tawanna, like you don't want me talkin' to your girl. Natalie, you know I'm just messin' with you, don't you? All jokes aside, you really do look good."

Natalie began to notice the other women whispering to each other and assumed that they had also figured out exactly who she was. She was the girl whose pregnancy had made the evening news. Now, thrust into the limelight once again, Natalie looked at Tawanna with teary eyes that apologized for making an appearance. Without saying a word, she got up and sprinted out.

"Wait!" Natalie heard Tawanna yell after her, but she didn't dare turn back.

It was close to eleven o'clock. After driving around for a while, Natalie had stumbled across the Blue Lounge. Though tempted to go in, she sat in her car and watched others come and go as the music blared from inside the bar. She'd sat there for at least an hour, wishing she had gone back to Columbus several days ago as she had originally planned.

A steady flow of tears swam down her face as she once again relived her horrific adolescent years. She wasn't sure whether Kya knew the particulars about her pregnancy, but she had to have sense enough to know it was a sensitive subject. Natalie wasn't "fast," as Kya had implied. Her virginity hadn't been given away…it had been taken by her stepfather when she was only ten years old.

Being molested formed the darkest period of Natalie's life. Like many children, she didn't tell anyone. She wondered if it was somehow her fault because Jesse always accused her of flaunting it at him. Night after night he had repeatedly snuck into Natalie's bedroom while her mother was asleep and stolen her virtue, being sure to reward her with gifts. There was nothing Natalie wanted that she didn't get. Jesse would often encourage her to use her body and looks to get anything she desired. Sadly, it was a lesson she carried well into adulthood.

It wasn't until a routine examination uncovered an eight-week pregnancy that Natalie was forced to admit everything. Her family was outraged, but Jesse was well known throughout the Jackson community as a politician and philanthropist. He had supporters who actually believed his concocted story that Natalie was nothing more than a teenage slut who'd gotten knocked up by some little boy at school and was afraid to tell the truth so she blamed him. To make matters worse, Jesse was never legally held accountable for his crime. He knew people in powerful positions who pulled strings and prevented charges from being brought against him. By the time their child was born, he'd left town. Natalie didn't know what had ever become of him. She secretly hoped he was somewhere dead and buried and unable to hurt anyone else.

She'd never understood how God, who was supposed to be this Great and Mighty Being, could let something like that happen to a child. Perhaps that unanswered question was what had kept her from seeking Him all this time. Though she still didn't understand, she couldn't deny how much better she felt having Him in her life. She sat in her car, thinking about the devotional she'd read that morning: Proverbs 3:5, "Trust in the Lord with all thine heart and lean not unto thine own understanding." She didn't know how He was going to do it, but somehow God had to help her through this.

Prior to Sunday, Natalie would have gone into the bar to drink and dance her sorrows away without any thought. Her hesitation was a sign that, even in a short amount of time, Jesus had made a difference in her life. *I'm a new creation in Christ,* she reminded herself and started her car while she was still strong enough to fight the temptation.

As she was about to drive off, she saw a familiar face come out of the bar seductively dressed in a tight red leather miniskirt, knee-length boots and a tank top that came off her shoulders. It was Corrine.

The young girl looked around as though she was searching for someone, then hung her head in despair, and took a seat at the bus stop. Natalie became concerned for Corrine's safety when she observed an older gentleman approach her. It appeared as though she refused an offer of some kind, but the guy remained persistent.

Natalie couldn't drive away in good conscience while Corrine got hassled. She drove a few feet ahead to the bus stop and rolled down the passenger window. "Do you want a ride?"

Corrine squinted her eyes, peering into Natalie's car. "Yes!" Her face brightened and she immediately got up from the bench, rushing by the older man.

"I take it you didn't know him?" Natalie asked after Corrine was secured inside the vehicle.

Corrine shook her head no. "He asked me if I was interested in going back to his place."

"I'm glad you didn't take him up on his offer. I'm sure he was up to no good. What were you doing at a bar anyhow?" she grilled, pulling away. "You're too young and it's very dangerous to be out alone this time of night."

"Thanks for the ride and all, but can you spare me the lecture? I'm already gonna have to hear my mama's mouth. The less people who tell me off, the better."

"My bad...I didn't mean to come at you harshly. It's just that you could've gotten hurt tonight. How'd you get into the bar, anyhow?"

"My roommate got me a fake ID," Corrine closed her eyes and laid her head back on the headrest. "Mama is going to kill me."

"If you promise never to go to that bar again, I promise I won't say anything to Aunt Toni about this."

Corrine's eyes popped open and she lifted her head. "Seriously?"

"Yeah, but you have to promise."

"I won't go again, I swear."

"Then it's a deal."

"Cool!" Corrine exclaimed, sitting straight up. "If it weren't for LaShina, I wouldn't have been there anyhow."

"Where do you want me to take you?"

"Back to campus."

"Who is LaShina?"

"My roommate. She's the one who left me stranded because she took off with some man. Supposedly, she was coming right back, but I haven't seen her. She won't even answer her cell phone. I've been sittin' in there for over an hour doing nothing. The whole night was her idea. I don't even drink. She begged me to come with her and then left me there by myself. She'd better not be at the dorm because I'm gonna strangle her if I see her tonight."

"I know you're angry, and you have every right to be, but I don't think it's a good idea that you go back to the dorm right now."

"I don't have any where else to go. I definitely don't want to go to my mama's house. I'll be all right. If LaShina's there, I won't kill her, but I'm going to let her know how I feel."

"You're liable to get yourself into some serious trouble if you confront her while you're upset. Why don't we go somewhere until you can calm down?"

"Fine, whatever." Corrine once again closed her eyes and put her head back.

Natalie drove around for a while, finally pulling into the parking lot of a late-night diner. She and Corrine went inside. Neither of them were hungry so they both ordered milkshakes—Corrine wanted a chocolate one and Natalie got strawberry. It was close to midnight and Natalie figured her grandmother would be worried about her so she looked inside her purse for her cell phone. "Aw, man…"

"What's wrong?" Corrine asked.

"I must've left my cell phone at Big Mama's. I was about to call her because I know she's probably wondering where I am. I'll be right back. I'm gonna see if I can find a pay phone."

"You can use mine," Corrine offered, extending her flip-top.

"Thanks." Natalie dialed her grandmother's number.

"Hello?"

"Hey, it's me."

"Are you all right?"

"Yes, I'm fine."

"Tawanna called and told me what happened at the shower. Baby, I'm so sorry Kya did that to you. I declare that chile has a few loose screws in her head. Tawanna and I have both been tryin' to get you on your cell phone."

"It must be at the house because it's not with me."

"Where are you at?"

"At a diner. I came here to chill for a minute. I figured you'd be wondering where I was. I just wanted you to know that I'm okay so you wouldn't be worried about me."

"You're comin' back tonight, aren't you?"

"Yes, I'll be there in a little while."

"You be careful. It's not safe for a young woman to be out by herself this time of night."

"I know, Big Mama. I'm fine. You go ahead and go to bed. Don't worry about trying to wait up for me. Didn't you say you had somewhere to be in the morning?"

"Yeah, it's my Saturday to help clean the church. But, I'm gonna call and switch days with somebody first thing in the mornin'. I really think it's time you and I talked about this. We've been avoiding it much too long."

"No, go to the church. Don't stay home on my account. I'm fine."

"No, you're not. You've pretended to be, but I know better. Tawanna told me how upset you were. It's time you knew—"

"Kya caught me off guard, that's all. Go to the church like you had planned. We'll talk when you get back, okay?"

"All right…I guess that'll work. Don't stay out too late. I know you're grown and live on your own and everything, but that don't mean I cain't be concerned about your safety."

"I promise I'll be there in a little while."

"Okay, you be careful now."

"I will."

"I love you…"

"I love you, too…. Here you go," she said, handing Corrine's phone back to her.

"Is everything fine?"

"Yeah."

"I feel sort of stupid because I don't know your name."

"Corrine, that's nothing to feel stupid about. We were never formally introduced. It's Natalie."

"I don't know what I would've done if you hadn't shown up at the bar. What were you doing down there anyway?"

"I…I was just riding around. I'm sorry that girl left you alone down there. How long have y'all known each other?"

"We just met this year at school although I doubt she'll be there next year, her grades are so bad. I know she's not the best influence for me. At first, she was just fun and cool to hang around. Then, I noticed little shady things she would do."

"Like what?"

"Just a bunch of small stuff, but still shady. One time I was going out with this boy named DeVonté and LaShina started going out with him behind my back. At first I was mad, but then I figured that boys aren't worth breaking a friendship over, right?"

"You're right, but if LaShina really valued you as a friend, she wouldn't have done that to you. It sounds to me like she has some security issues. You can be the best friend in the world to her, but if she has insecurities, she's liable to do lots of things that will hurt you. It doesn't necessarily mean that she's a bad person. Maybe there's some things that happened in her childhood that have screwed up her way of thinking and she's handling her friendships the best way she knows how to right now."

"Maybe…" Corrine shrugged.

"In any event, I think your best bet is not to get emotionally tied up with her because if she does have a lot of junk going on in her life, she'll end up hurting herself and you. She either has some serious undealt-with issues, or she's just crazy. Either way, stay away from her."

"Are you some type of psychologist or something?"

"No."

"You sound like it."

"Let's just say that I've had some LaShina experiences before."

Corrine sipped on her shake with a distant look in her eyes. "Can I ask you a question without offending you?"

"Sure," Natalie said, hoping the question wouldn't be anything too personal.

"Are you really Big Mama's granddaughter?"

"Yeah, why do you ask me that?"

"I was just wondering because I know there are some folks that call her Big Mama who aren't really related to her and I've never seen you before."

"Do you know Uncle Willie?"

"Yes, but I know you aren't his daughter 'cuz he got all sons."

"Well, my father, James, was Uncle Willie's twin brother. Have you ever seen the picture on Big Mama's piano of a little girl with long hair, wearing a blue-and-white polka-dot dress?"

"Yeah, I think I know what picture you're referring to."

"That's me."

"Oh, okay! I remember asking Big Mama about that picture one time because it reminded me of one of my childhood pictures. She told me that your dad was killed in a car accident, was it?"

"Yeah, he was. It was a long time ago so you wouldn't have known him. I was only five back then."

"Dang, I'm sorry to hear that. Is that why you moved?"

"No. My mother and I actually lived here until I was thirteen, then we moved to Ohio with my mom's best friend."

"My mama has a friend that lives in Ohio."

"Let me guess, are you talking about Sylvia Turner?"

"Yeah, you know her?"

"Yep, I sure do. She's who we moved up there to live with. She and Aunt Crystal grew up with my dad, Aunt Toni, Uncle Tommy—all of them."

"Yeah, my mama told me. Why haven't you ever come for holidays or family reunions?"

"There've been a lot of reasons. The important thing is that I'm here now." Natalie quickly sought to turn the conversation away from her and back to Corrine. "You're a freshman in college, right?"

"Yeah…"

"What's your major?"

"I haven't really declared a major, but it's either going to be music or marketing."

"Those are very different fields. How'd you come up with that?"

"I'm really interested in marketing, but I love to sing."

"I bet you inherited singing from Big Mama. I wish I could sing, but I took after my mother who couldn't hold a note to save her life."

Corrine sat quiet, stirring her straw in her shake.

"You okay?"

"Yeah…" She looked sad. "I wish I could say I inherited my singing skills from Big Mama. Truth is, I don't know where I got it from."

"True, but does anyone ever *really* know? Who's to say that you didn't inherit it from her? Big Mama got some pipes. I do know that for a fact."

"How can you inherit something from a woman you're not biologically related to?"

Natalie felt like a complete idiot having forgotten that Toni was her stepmother. "I'm sorry. I wasn't thinking when I said that. But I'm sure you know that Big Mama has a huge heart. I bet she loves you as if you *were* her biological granddaughter."

"Yeah, but it still sucks not knowing who I belong to."

"I take it that you don't have a relationship with your real mother."

"No, I don't…I don't have a relationship with either one of my biological parents."

Natalie's confusion must have shown on her face.

"I'm adopted," Corrine explained.

"I realize Aunt Toni adopted you, but I thought she married your father. She told me that he had children before the two of them married."

"Correction…he didn't have children, he had *a* child, Li'l Kenny."

"I don't understand."

"What's not to understand? I was given up for adoption by my birth mother and my mama—your Aunt Toni—adopted me. Sometimes I fantasize about what my life would be like if my real parents had kept me, but then I feel bad because I know my mama made a lot of sacrifices for me. I hear she was on her way to becoming one of the greatest attorneys in Jackson, but then she chose me over her career. As much as my mama gets on my nerves, I can't honestly say that many single women would have done what she did."

"Are you saying that Aunt Toni adopted you before she and your father were married?"

"Yeah. I think she met my dad when I was like two or something. After they got married, he adopted me, too."

Goosebumps burst through Natalie's skin as she carefully dissected Corrine's words. "Has Aunt Toni ever told you anything about your biological mother? Were they friends perhaps? I mean, I'm just trying to figure out why Aunt Toni would adopt you when it sounds like she had a very promising career ahead of her. Not saying that she shouldn't have. I'm curious about what led her to that decision."

Corrine shrugged. "You know, I really don't know the circumstances. I suspect that she had to know of my biological mother, but I'm not sure she knew her. Whenever I would ask about my birth mother, Mama would say that it was a young girl she wanted to help out. That's all she ever told me. Finally I gave up and quit asking. It's probably for the best. If my biological mother would give me up for adoption then odds are she didn't want me anyhow."

Natalie's heart raced. Could Corrine be her child? She had to be certain. "When is your birthday?" she asked, casually.

Corrine looked at her as if to say "What does that have to do with anything?" but answered. "July twenty-ninth…"

Natalie almost choked on her shake and her breath grew heavy. She struggled with what to say next. She was sure she was staring at the face of her daughter!

Corrine looked strangely at Natalie, whose expression was probably that of someone who had seen a ghost. Natalie thought she was about to say something else, but then Corrine's cell phone rang. "Hello?…What do you mean where am I? Where were you when I was about to get kidnapped at the Blue Lounge?"

Natalie stared as Corrine talked, paying more attention to her features. She'd never noticed the color of Corrine's eyes before, but they were copper brown and narrow, just like her own. Her hair—her hair was silky and long—just like Natalie's. The more she looked at Corrine, the more she saw herself.

"Why did you take off with some dude and leave me at the bar alone?" Corrine rolled her eyes. "Whatever…I'll see you when I see you." She hung up the phone. "I can't believe that girl! She had the nerve to show back up at the bar finally then call goin' off on me because I'm not there waiting on her. Can you take me back to the dorm now? LaShina isn't coming back tonight. She said she was going to spend the night with her cousin."

"Um…sure. Just let me go to the bathroom first." Natalie pulled out a ten-dollar bill from her purse. "Can you go ahead and pay? I'll meet you in the front." Natalie got up from the table and went to the restroom. With her heart pounding against her chest and her head spinning, she leaned over the bathroom sink as though she would vomit. She was in shock. She splashed cold water on her face and took several deep breaths before going back out.

"Do you mind showing me where your parents live before I take you to the school?" Natalie asked once they were in the car.

"What do you want to go over there for?" Corrine seemed skeptical.

"I need to talk to your mother about something."

"You're not backing out from our deal, are you?"

"No. I told you that I won't tell her about tonight. We made a pact and I intend to keep my promise," Natalie declared. "I just want to talk to her before I leave town and I don't know where she stays." Seeming a little uncertain, Corrine showed her the way.

Chapter 30

A Family Matter

Natalie got back to the house and discovered that her grandmother had fallen asleep in the living-room recliner. Instead of waking her, Natalie crept past Big Mama and up to her room. She tossed and turned during the night. If what she thought was true, *everyone*, including Big Mama, had to know.

The next morning, Natalie pretended to be asleep until her grandmother left and then headed to Toni's house where she was determined not to leave until all of her questions were answered. As she neared the front door of her aunt's two-story brick home, her stomach churned with fear. What if her suspicions were wrong? What if Corrine's birthday was some freak coincidence? She couldn't say for sure that her child had been a girl. What if she was just setting herself up for another letdown like the one she'd had when she'd called the adoption agencies thinking she would get answers. Natalie wasn't sure how many more disappointments she could take and still keep what little sanity she had left. Yet, the burning desire for clarity prompted her to knock on the door, and she did so, despite her trembling hands.

"Can I help you?" a young boy answered.

"Hi, is your mother home?"

"Zach, who is it?" Natalie heard Toni yell from the background.

"It's that lady that was with Big Mama at church."

"What lady?" Antoinette rounded the corner and paused when she saw Natalie. "Zachary, go back to whatever it was you were doing. I got it from here," she said, coldly. "What are you doing here?"

"I'm leaving in a couple of days and I really haven't talked to you much since I've been here. I thought I would come by and visit before I went back to Columbus."

"Now really isn't a good time. My son has a basketball game in a few hours. Maybe I can come by and see you later this afternoon at Mama's house."

Like that was really going to happen! Toni had yet to come by the home since she'd been there. "I probably should've called first, but I didn't have your number. Since I'm here, I might as well come in and visit for a few moments…just in case we both get busy later."

"I… Sure, why not?" Toni grudgingly stepped aside, making a small entry way for Natalie to enter.

"You have a nice house." She took a seat on the sofa, hearing the sound of video games and music coming from upstairs.

"Thanks." Toni sat in the chair across from her, stiffly.

"How long have you lived here?"

"We bought this house about twelve years ago when we moved from Louisiana."

"I didn't know you used to live there."

"Just for a few years…. Does Mama know you're here?"

Toni asked as if she was concerned that Big Mama had orchestrated this visit.

"No. She was gone when I got up. She went to clean the church."

"How'd you know where I lived?"

Natalie thought about saying that she'd looked up the address in the telephone book, but realized that she didn't even know her aunt's married name. Also, what if Toni's number wasn't listed in the phone book? Lying about how she obtained the information could backfire against her. Instead of answering Toni's question, she asked a direct one of her own. "Does my being here bother you?"

"Should it?"

"I don't know. You tell me. I get the impression that you've been avoiding me."

Toni laughed nervously. "Why in the world would I do that?"

"That's what I'm trying to understand. You seemed very cold when I answered the phone at Big Mama's that day you called, and you left the table rather quickly when I spoke to you at Uncle Tommy's celebration last Sunday."

"I think you're being a little too sensitive...or paranoid. It was quite a shock to call my mama's house and have you answer the phone. I wasn't expecting that. And as far as last Sunday goes, I do recall introducing you to my husband and talkin' with you for a while, so I'm not sure why you would feel that way. You know, I wish I could be more hospitable, but we really do have a hectic day ahead of us. I'll be happy to walk you to your car." She stood up.

"Why are you so uncomfortable with me here?" Natalie challenged, remaining in her seat.

Toni turned her back toward Natalie, appearing to straighten the pictures on her mantel, and giving what seemed like another nervous laugh. "That's silly. There's no reason for me to be uncomfortable in my own home. I think you're the one who's uncomfortable, which is all the more reason why you should leave."

"I'll leave…but first I have to ask you something."

"What can I help you with?"

"Why would a young, single woman—who had a promising career ahead of her—give it all up to adopt a baby?"

One of the pictures toppled. "I'm not sure I know what you mean."

"That's interesting, considering the fact that you adopted Corrine."

"Who told you that?" Toni turned around and barked.

"It doesn't matter. I just want to know one thing…" Natalie stood up and walked a few feet and looked her aunt directly in the eye. "Is Corrine my daughter?"

Toni rolled her eyes. "You're crazy."

"Toni, cut the crap and tell me the truth!"

"How dare you come into my home and be disrespectful to me."

"I just want to know about Corrine."

"Well, I'm sorry, but the topic of Corrine is off limits."

"Why…because she's really *my* child?"

Toni glared at her. "You listen to me very carefully. Make no mistakes about it. Corrine is *my* daughter. I'm the one who sacrificed my life to raise her. For all intents and purposes, I *am* her mother and that is *all* that you need to know."

"Here's a news flash, Toni— What happened to me as a child was tragic. A person doesn't just get over that. Don't you think I deserve to know that truth?"

"Oh, so that's what Corrine is to you, a tragedy? Kenny and I don't look at her as a tragic event in our lives. We see a young girl, full of potential, who can be anything in this world she wants to be. I'm sorry for what happened to you, Natalie, but there's nothin' I can do about it, is there?"

"The least you can do is tell Corrine who I really am."

"Why? What good would that do? Then she'll want to know the circumstances surrounding her birth. How would it benefit her to know she's a product of sexual molestation?"

"She wants to know!" Natalie screamed. "She thinks I didn't want her."

Toni looked horrified. "You've spoken to Corrine about this?"

Realizing she'd put herself in an awkward position of disclosure, Natalie didn't respond.

"You'd better stay away from her. If anyone is going to tell Corrine anything, it'll be me or her father. This is a family matter and does not concern you! You haven't thought about seeing her the last eighteen years, why now? Is it because you're trying to ease your own conscience about giving her up?"

"I was a child! I didn't have a choice. My mother made me!"

"Yeah, well, Sharon knew that I had Corrine all along and she never came down to lay eyes on her."

"You liar! Don't you dare make it seem like my mother was involved in this." Before Natalie could catch herself she'd slapped Toni right in the middle of her cheek.

Toni quickly massaged the point of impact, fire blazing in her eyes. "If you think Sharon was ignorant of this whole deal, think again. The whole thing was her idea—including not telling you."

"Shut up! You're lying. My mother would've never kept something like this from me."

Toni laughed wickedly. "Why do you think y'all moved to Ohio so quickly? Earl and Crystal were going to raise Corrine, but Earl had reservations about all the secrecy. I, on the other hand, agreed with your mother and thought it would be best for everyone involved. Face it, Natalie. Your mother never wanted you to know where Corrine was. Why else would she have taken this secret with her to the grave?"

Natalie shook her head. "No…this can't be true."

"Your best bet is to go back to Columbus, New York, or wherever you want to go and forget that Corrine ever existed. You should be able to get over Corrine, Sharon did!" Toni's sharp words pierced Natalie's heart.

"I will *never* forget Corrine!" she declared, then turned and burst through the front door, almost knocking Toni's husband over as he was coming in.

Natalie drove around for a while trying to calm her nerves before going back to her grandmother's. When she arrived, Big Mama and Crystal were both in the living room waiting for her. Their troubled expressions told Natalie that they'd already been informed about the morning's events. "I'm gonna get my things and then I'll be going home," she stated and proceeded to her room.

"Wait…" Her grandmother gently grabbed her arm. "I wanna talk to you."

Ordering her tears not to fall, Natalie said, "I'd rather not. No one wanted to talk to me about Corrine for the past eighteen and a half years. I don't want to talk now."

Natalie burst into tears when she entered her room. She felt betrayed by everyone in her family—especially by her deceased mother and her grandmother. How could they have kept such an important thing from her? Their deceitfulness was totally unforgivable.

"Do you mind if I say something?" Crystal came into the room.

"I don't feel like talking to you or anyone else."

"You don't have to say a word, just listen to me, please…"

Natalie continued shoving her belongings into her bag.

"Honey, I know you're hurting right now. I just don't think you should try and drive all that way being so upset. If you don't want to stay here, you're welcome to come to my house."

"No, thanks."

"Everyone is upset right now. Kenny said Toni is hysterical and about to have a nervous breakdown."

"Ask me if I care…"

"Your grandmother is torn to pieces. Natalie, she loves you *so* much. When I picked her up to go to the church this morning, she told me what happened last night at Tawanna's bridal shower. She had her mind set that if you wanted to know the truth, she was going to tell you and deal with the repercussions from Toni later."

"I can't really hold her accountable for not telling me anything during the years we didn't talk much. But, we've talked to each other at least once a week for well over a year now since my mom died. She's had plenty of time to tell me if she really wanted to, so how likely is it that she would have told me today?" Natalie yelled. "I've been here two weeks and she hasn't said a word."

"I understand how you feel. I—"

"No, you don't! You don't know how it feels to wake up in the middle of the night and cry because you don't know who or where your child is. You don't know how it feels to find out that your mother kept the truth from you all along, going on like nothing ever happened. You don't know how it feels to have a miscarriage that hurt so bad it felt like losing Corrine all over again. I came to Mississippi trying to find answers about my past. The funny thing is that everyone who knew the answers looked me in my face and no one had the decency to tell me. Unless you've been through that, you don't know how I feel so I'd appreciate if you would move out of my way."

Crystal stepped aside as Natalie rushed out the room.

"Please don't leave like this," her grandmother desperately pleaded.

"Goodbye," Natalie quietly said, refusing to look at her.

Chapter 31

A Grain of Salt

After driving straight from Jackson to Columbus, Natalie was mentally and physically tired by the time she got to her apartment. She lay in bed Sunday morning recapping the last two weeks of her life and feeling overwhelmed by such widespread betrayal by her family. On the one hand, it felt good finally to know the truth. On the other, she believed that had she known all along, many of her emotional and social dysfunctions could have been avoided. She was now stuck with knowing the truth, but not really knowing how to process it and get on with her life.

"Natalie, please open up!" It was about a quarter after nine when Sylvia came banging at the door. "I know you're in there. I saw your car outside," she yelled.

Since it didn't sound as if Sylvia would leave anytime soon, Natalie crawled out of bed and went to the door. "What?"

Sylvia took it upon herself to fully invite herself into the apartment. "Are you okay?"

"Hmm… What would make you ask that? Is it because Big Mama or Crystal called and told you that I found out about Corrine? I'm sure you already knew—just like everyone else."

"Natalie, Ida Mae is worried sick about you."

"Then call and tell her I'm fine."

"I think she would much rather hear it from you."

"Tough! I don't want to talk to her. I don't even want to talk to you."

"Nat, I know you're upset, but you have to believe that no one intentionally tried to hurt you."

Natalie rolled her eyes and leaned against the wall. "Yeah, well I'm sure Toni would disagree."

"I haven't spoken to her about what happened between y'all, but I'm willing to bet that even she feels bad for whatever she said."

"What I don't understand, Sylvia, is how everyone could think that having a baby was something I could just forget about." She began tearing up.

"Oh, honey, no one thought you forgot—"

"Then why wouldn't anyone tell me that Toni had my baby? Why didn't you tell me? My own mother didn't even say anything!" Natalie exploded.

Sylvia remained calm. "When you guys first moved up here, Sharon told me that she didn't want you to know who had Corrine because she feared it would be harder for you to move on in life. She specifically said that the only way she would tell you everything was if you asked. It's my understanding that you never asked. I'm not blaming you at all, I'm just trying to get you to understand that Sharon thought you were okay with not knowing. You seemed to be getting along great in high school, you graduated from college and you were modeling in New York…you seemed very happy. Sharon didn't want to take any of that away from you. If she thought for one minute that you wanted to know about Corrine, she would have told you."

"Toni made it sound as if Mom never wanted to lay eyes on Corrine."

"Take anything Toni said about Sharon with a grain of salt," Sylvia said angrily. "Your mother did what she thought was best to do at the time, but it wasn't an easy decision for her by any means. She wanted to keep Corrine, but honestly didn't have the financial means to care for you and a baby. She longed to see Corrine. As a matter of fact, she cried when she saw the pictures that Toni would send me of her. Toni was just running off at the mouth because she's battling her own fears."

"I just want the pain to stop," Natalie cried. "I just want it to stop."

"Honey, it will. It'll take time, but it will." Sylvia hugged her tightly.

It was well after ten o'clock when Sylvia left. She tried to talk Natalie into getting dressed and going to get something to eat with her, but Natalie didn't have an appetite and didn't feel like company. She briefly considered visiting one of the churches on the list that Earl had given her just to get her mind on something else, but at the rate she was moping around, she'd never make it to any of the services on time. She spent the entire day in bed, watching Lifetime and ignoring the phone each time it rang.

Later on that night Natalie read two of her daily devotions, catching up on what she'd missed yesterday because of all the drama that had taken place. Afterwards, she decided to try her hand at praying. Besides the day Earl had led her in the prayer of salvation, she hadn't really ventured into that territory on her own. It was easy to pray when all she had to do was repeat after her uncle. Still, she'd give it a try.

"Dear God…um…I hope You can hear me…I'm hurting, and I'm not sure how to deal with everything. I really want to be saved and be a good Christian. Please quiet the voices in my head that tell me I'm going to fail at Christianity like I've failed at modeling, friendships, relationships and would've most likely failed at motherhood, which is probably why I miscarried, huh? I know I can't do this without You, so please help me. Oh, and one more thing…please take care of Corrine."

Chapter 32

Nosey By Nature

Natalie woke up way too early the next morning. She still had at least an hour before she would normally get up for work. Surprisingly, she was feeling a little better than she had the day before, though the whole situation still bothered her quite a bit. Realizing her mind was too active to allow her to go back to sleep, she turned on the lamp and opened her devotional book.

Immediately her flesh warmed when she saw today's title: "Learning to Forgive." The devotion was based on Matthew 18: 21-35 when Jesus told Peter a parable about a king who forgave one of his servants of an insurmountable debt. The same servant was owed less money by someone else, but instead of forgiving him, had the person thrown in prison when he could not pay. The king found out what the servant had done and was filled with anger. The king ordered the jailers to torture him until he could pay off the entire debt owed to the king. At the end of the parable Jesus said, "This is how my heavenly Father will treat each of you unless you forgive your brother from your heart."

The author of the devotion then wrote, "Where would you be if God refused to forgive you?" The message wasn't easy for Natalie to digest because she felt she had a *right* to be angry with everyone. There was a whole list of people who had violated her trust. How could she ever forgive Jesse! The man had stolen her innocence! Yet, as the writer pointed out, forgiveness was not optional, but a necessity.

Natalie finally understood what Wendy had said the day they'd run into each other at Babies "R" Us. Wendy had stated that she *had* to forgive Natalie in order to be right with God. Forgiveness is a Christ-like characteristic.

In addition to forgiving others, Natalie also had to forgive herself for all the wrong choices she had made in her life-time. She'd been using her childhood as a crutch to justify her behavior. Though she might not have been able to prevent the things that had happened to her as a child, she did have a choice in how she responded to them later in life. Jesse had stolen her virginity, but she had later willingly given her goodness away to dozens of other men. Death had halted the relationship she'd had with her father, but it was her own avoidance that had prevented meaningful relation-ships with friends and family.

Startled when the alarm clock blared at six, signifying she should start getting ready for work, Natalie picked up the phone and dialed her grandmother's number. Though it was only five o'clock in Jackson, she didn't want to let an-other minute go by without making an effort to mend their broken relationship. She already lived with the regret about not being there for her mother. She knew that if something were to happen to Big Mama, she would hate herself for allowing her fierce departure from Mississippi to be the last interaction that the two of them had. Natalie waited with anticipation as her grandmother's phone rang. "Sorry to call you so early, I—"

"Baby, it's okay. It's not like I was gettin' much rest anyhow. I'm so glad you called. I tried gettin' a hold of you several times yesterday."

"I was here. I just didn't answer the phone. Sylvia came by for a minute."

"I know… How are you doing?"

"Okay…I guess I could be a lot worse. My whole purpose for coming to Mississippi was to find out what had happened to my baby. I just can't understand why no one would tell me."

"Baby, I'm so sorry. I didn't know…" Hearing the tearful plea in her grandmother's voice caused tears to well up in Natalie's own eyes. "You seemed to make it very clear that you didn't want to talk about what happened back then. I guess it was just easier for me not to push the issue. I knew if I told you, Toni would have a fit. She's my only daughter and I was scared of damaging our relationship."

"But Crystal said you were going to tell me Saturday…."

"After I got the phone call from Tawanna about you runnin' out of the bridal shower, I called Toni and said that I would tell you about Corrine. Of course, she was livid, but I wanted to do what I thought was right."

"That must be why Toni wondered if you knew I was going over to her house… I take it Tawanna knows, too."

"She overheard me and Bessie talkin' one time. Please don't be upset with her. She found out by mistake. She couldn't have been more than sixteen at the time."

Natalie couldn't reasonably be upset with Tawanna even if she had wanted to be. Of all the people involved in this conspiracy, she was the last one who should've felt obligated to come clean. "Has anyone told Corrine who I am?"

"No. Toni was afraid that her other children had overheard you two, but so far none of them have said anything. Personally, I think everything needs to come out in the open, but I will not tell Corrine. I respect Toni as her mother and whether or not Corrine is told the truth needs to be her decision. I've given her my opinion, but the rest is up to her."

"I guess you're right…." Though she desired for Corrine to know, she really had no say-so.

"Natalie, I *am* sorry."

"I am, too. I should've at least tried to talk to you instead of blowing up."

"I cain't honestly say that I wouldn't have done the same thing if I were you. We're all human, sometimes our emotions get the best of us."

"Thank you for being so understanding. I love you, Big Mama."

"I love you, too, baby."

Natalie looked at the clock. It was already after six-thirty. "I'd better get off the phone so I can get to work. I wanted to be there early this morning since it's my first day back, but it doesn't look like that's going to happen."

"Okay. Do you mind if I pray with you real quick?"

Natalie smiled for the first time since she'd been back in Columbus. "Of course not," she said and closed her eyes in anticipation.

The best part of Natalie's first day back at work was the exuberant and warm greeting from Aneetra, who was eager to hear all about her trip. Natalie felt as though she could trust Aneetra with her secret, but the hectic workday left no time for full disclosure—perhaps tomorrow when they went to lunch. She was taking Aneetra out as a way to say "thank you" for handling her workload and helping to smooth things over with Alex, who initially had been very upset that Natalie hadn't called her while she was away. She had become more sympathetic upon learning about the miscarriage, however.

As promised, Natalie had phoned Troy to let him know she was back in town, and now she sat on her couch waiting for his arrival. It was a few minutes shy of seven when he knocked on the door. He stood before her smiling, looking way sexier than she remembered him to be.

Stepping in, he squeezed her between his arms, gently kissing her forehead. "I'm glad you're back." She was searching for the proper words to greet him, but her thoughts were interrupted by his lips, causing a serious flutter in her stomach. "I'm sorry for the way I've acted…. Can you forgive me?"

"I already have." She stared into his heartfelt gaze.

"I have something that belongs to you." He let Natalie go and reached into his back pocket, pulling out his wallet, and handed her a folded sheet of paper.

She didn't have to unfold the paper to know that it was the poem she'd written after she'd had the miscarriage. "Thanks for giving it back to me. This is very personal, you know?"

"I do, and I'm sorry for invading your privacy."

"No, you're not," she teased. "Detectives are never sorry about that, you guys are nosey by nature."

Troy laughed. "You might be right about that."

"Go ahead and have a seat. I'm gonna go put this inside my desk this time." She headed to the spare bedroom where her computer was located. Just as she had shoved the poem underneath some papers and closed the drawer, Troy's arms engulfed her from behind. She hadn't heard him come into the room.

"I do love you," he whispered.

His words melted her heart, overshadowing the damage he'd previously done to it. She turned to face him. "I love you, too," she managed to squeeze out before their lips were drawn together again. The more intense the kiss got, the more her body craved his touch. *Wait! We can't do this!* her conscience cried, but Natalie was unable to force the words from her head out of her mouth. Troy's lips held hers captive.

He scooped Natalie up in his arms and carried her to the master bedroom where they fell on top of her comforter. She assisted him with pulling his sweatshirt over his head and immediately began kissing his chest. Troy moaned with pleasure and Natalie's body began reacting to the anticipation of being pleasured. She wanted him badly, but her conscience began troubling her when he attempted to unbutton her shirt, and scriptures she'd read during her devotions last week floated through her head.

Natalie saw the hunger in his eyes for her and her appetite was just as ferocious. *I am a new creation,* her conscience refused to be silent. Torn between her newly-developed spiritual discipline and the lusting of her flesh, she gave in. "I can't do this…" She pushed him off and jumped out of bed, refastening the few buttons he'd undone while she could still think straight.

"What?"

"I'm sorry…I just got caught up in the moment, but I can't go through with this."

"Baby, what's wrong?" He got up and gently held her shoulders.

"Nothing… It's not you…I promise. Just please…*please* put your shirt back on." She charged out of the bedroom.

Troy soon followed behind her, leaving his sweatshirt behind. "Nat, what's going on? Talk to me, please. Did I do something?"

"No, this has nothing to do with you. It's me."

"Are you scared that you'll get pregnant again? Honestly, I am. That's why I think we should use protection. Our relationship has a lot of healing to go through yet and we should be careful."

"I…I really can't talk to you about this right now." Natalie was still fighting her desire for him and seeing his sculpted chest didn't make things any easier. She needed him to leave quickly before she found herself back in the bedroom, completing the mission. "Please go put your shirt on and leave."

"Natalie…"

"*Please* just go…We'll talk later, I promise."

Troy sighed heavily. "I don't understand you…" He stormed off back into her bedroom for his shirt and minutes later left the apartment.

Chapter 33

It's About Me

"Wow, you really have been through a lot," Aneetra said to Natalie the next day as they ate lunch at a restaurant near where they worked. While enjoying her garlic shrimp platter across from Aneetra with her parmesan chicken, Natalie had just shared her discovery about Corrine.

"I know. It's a wonder I haven't lost my mind," Natalie replied, dipping one of her shrimp into the buttery sauce before bringing it to her mouth.

"For what it's worth, I think you're handling everything very well...I admire your strength. I can't honestly say that I would've left without telling Corrine the truth, but I do think you did the right thing. It really should be your aunt's decision whether she finds out."

"I doubt that will ever happen. If Toni had her way, I'm sure she'd want me as far from Mississippi as possible. I'm willing to bet that Columbus isn't far enough. She'd probably ship me off to Asia or somewhere if she could."

"I agree with your friend, Sylvia. Sounds to me like your aunt is dealing with her own fears."

"Truthfully, I think Corrine was better off with Toni than if my mom had allowed me to keep her. I was thirteen—the whole situation was crazy, you know? I don't think either my mom or I would have been emotionally strong enough to raise a child under those circumstances. It's not like I want to replace Toni as Corrine's mother. I would just like the opportunity to get to know her—for us to build some kind of relationship together. We seemed to really gel that night we talked."

"Just because your aunt says she doesn't want to tell her now, it doesn't mean she never will. You said your grandmother agrees that Corrine should be told the truth. I'm sure your uncles probably do, too. It's not likely that your aunt really has a whole lot of backing on this issue. Give her time, she'll come around."

"Yeah, well I'm not gonna hold my breath…"

"What does Troy have to say about everything?"

"Well…I haven't really told him."

Aneetra seemed surprised. "Oh…"

"Honestly, I'm scared. I'm afraid he might freak out like he did when I told him I was pregnant."

"Corrine and your pregnancy are two unrelated issues. I think you should tell him."

"I just don't know. What if, by some miracle, Corrine is able to be part of my life? *If* that ever happens, I'm not convinced that Troy will be accepting of that."

"You don't know that for sure. Give him a chance. Don't make the decision for him."

"Maybe… Right now wouldn't be a good time to tell him anyhow, things got a bit tense between us last night."

"What happened?" Aneetra asked just as Natalie's cell phone rang.

"Speak of the devil…"

"Well…are you gonna answer it?"

"Now is not the time."

"I don't know what happened with y'all last night, but I do know that you won't be able to avoid him forever. Troy has shown that he's willing to use any means possible to track you down. Please don't make the brotha start callin' me or camping out at folks' jobs again," she teased.

Laughing, Natalie reluctantly answered.

"Is this a bad time?" Troy asked.

"Sort of. I'm having lunch right now with Aneetra."

"Sorry, I won't hold you. Can we get together later this evening and talk? I'm confused about last night. I'm just trying to figure out where we stand. I promise I won't try anything else, but I really think we need to discuss some things."

"I agree…"

"So, do you want me to come to your place or do you want to come to mine?" he asked.

"How about we meet at Applebee's? I was gonna have to eat out tonight anyhow if I didn't get to the grocery store. I can get groceries tomorrow."

"I don't seem to have much of an appetite, but I guess that's cool. What time should we meet? Four-thirty?" he questioned.

"Yes, that's fine," Natalie stated. "I'll see you later."

"What happened with y'all last night?" Aneetra asked when Natalie had hung up.

"Let's just say that when the plane was about to land, I shut down the runway."

"Say no more, I know exactly what you mean…I've been there myself and, girl, it ain't easy."

"As much as I wanted to, I couldn't go through with it. Honest to God, I've never felt guilty about having premarital sex until last night."

"Girl, that's conviction. Now that you're saved, God's not going to make it easy for you to do wrong."

"I wish He would go ahead and take my desire away then because I really wanted him."

"Lesson number one—be careful what you pray for. Girl, you don't want God taking away your desire. Maybe ask Him to tone it down a little for the time being, but you definitely don't want it to be extinct. Trust me, you'll exercise it regularly one day." She winked. "That's an area many single Christians struggle with. I did. There was even one time when I failed to say no." Aneetra shook her head as though she was trying to erase an image from her mind. "I had been saved close to a year at the time. I have to be honest with you, Natalie. It wasn't worth it. Yeah, it felt good for the moment, but the guilt afterwards was unbearable."

Natalie appreciated her friend's candidness about this, as she had about the abortion. It put to rest those voices about Aneetra's life being "perfect" and made her realize that everyone has struggles.

"Thank God that there's forgiveness even when we're saved and we mess up. After that, I learned to keep myself out of predicaments where it would be easy for me to fall into temptation. I don't care how close the plane got to landing, I commend you for being able to stop it."

Natalie pulled into Applebee's parking lot about five minutes to five. She spotted Troy's Navigator and rushed in, finding that he'd already been seated.

"Sorry, I stayed at work a little longer than I'd planned to," she said, joining him at the booth.

"It's okay."

A blond waitress came up and, both claiming not to have much of an appetite, they ordered a raspberry iced tea for Natalie and a soda for Troy.

Yolonda Tonette Sanders

"Okay, I'll get those drinks right to you. If you change your minds about ordering just let me know," the waitress bubbled, leaving them alone.

"What happened last night?" Troy wasted no time getting to the point.

"I just couldn't go through with it."

"Why? Did you hook up with someone else in Mississippi? If so, let me know. Don't play games with me, Natalie. I'm trying my best to be open with you. I need you to do the same."

"This isn't about me finding anyone else."

"Then what is it about? Things seemed like they were going good then all of a sudden you flipped."

"I know, and I'm sorry about that. When I was in Mississippi, I made a decision to change my life. I got saved. As much as I wanted to be with you last night, doing so would have violated the commitment I'd made to Jesus."

"You are kidding me, right?" Troy looked amused. The waitress returned with their drinks, and, after she left, he continued. "Are you still upset with me because of how I reacted to your pregnancy? You know I'm sorry for the way I treated you. I tried to get you to understand where I was coming from."

"This has nothing to do with my pregnancy. Please don't think I'm holding anything against you. I really do forgive you. I'm sorry I let things get out of control last night. I got caught up in the moment. My decision not to follow through with things was based solely on me wanting to live the rest of my life as a Christian. It had absolutely nothing to do with what had happened between us previously. It's about my relationship with God."

"Are you going through some kind of identity crisis or something?" Troy began getting angry. "We've known each other for, like, ten months, and I have never heard you mention God except when cursing."

"You're right. I can't argue with that. But things have changed now. I made a commitment with my life and I intend to do my very best to follow through with it."

"So, how does our relationship fit in with your newfound commitment to God?"

Natalie's heart ached. There was no way she could confide in him about Corrine if he couldn't handle this. "I don't know," she said, fighting back tears. "Maybe we should try being friends and take things more slowly."

"So it's like that? You go to Mississippi as my girl, but come back and just wanna be my friend?"

"Troy, I just have a lot on my mind right now. I'm trying to put my life in perspective. I need to pursue my relationship with God if for no other reason than my own sanity."

"So what am I supposed to do while you and God are getting to know one another?" he mocked. "Do you expect me to feel the same way you do? I can tell you right now that I'm not on all of that going-to-church and reading-the-Bible stuff."

"I don't expect you to do anything you don't want to do. This isn't about us, Troy. It's about me and my relationship with God. I'm not trying to force you to do anything."

"I don't get it…it's like you're a totally different person. You know what? Thanks for the offer to be my friend, but I'll pass. You're not the person I fell in love with. I guess I won't be needing this any more." He threw her apartment key on the table before stomping away.

It was the second time a guy had walked out on her at a restaurant. At least she had the money to pay the bill this time.

Chapter 34

Making Right Your Wrongs

Over the next several weeks, Natalie tried to keep herself busy with work and other activities. Her personal schedule was often free and clear since she and Troy were no longer dating. She missed him and hadn't spoken with him in nearly six weeks, not since the day he'd walked out on her at the restaurant. Once she sent him an e-mail asking how he was doing, but didn't get a response. She'd been tempted many times to pick up the phone and call him, but had always decided against it, unsure of what emotions her actions would incite. Every now and then she would pray for him, hoping that whatever challenges life brought his way, he'd be able to handle.

Natalie was growing more confident in her ability to pray and she did so each day. One thing was for sure, God wouldn't find fault with her for padding her prayers with a lot of insincere murmurings. She stuck to the basics and made sure to include at least Big Mama and Corrine in every prayer. Through her grandmother, she had been able to keep tabs on what was going on with her daughter. Whether Toni ever decided to tell Corrine the truth or not, knowing Corrine was okay gave Natalie peace about the whole situation.

"Ugh!" Natalie grunted, crumpling the paper she had been writing on and throwing it on the floor alongside the rest. For the fourth time now, she was about to start her letter to Wendy, putting into practice the message that Aneetra's pastor had taught earlier today. Since her return from Mississippi, Natalie had been consistently attending her friend's church and was enjoying it. Today's message was probably the most challenging one she'd heard thus far, because it required her to take action.

Pastor Giles had preached a sermon entitled, "Making Right Your Wrongs," stating that it's part of our Christian responsibility to go back to the person we've offended and ask for forgiveness. He warned the congregation to remember that asking forgiveness doesn't undo the past, nor does it make the other person's pain go away. He said that people need time to heal and they must be allowed whatever time is necessary. Finally, he mentioned that even when people apologize, they can't make others forgive them. The reality is that sometimes people will never forgive, but fear of rejection doesn't negate the offender's responsibility.

Though extremely grateful to have both Aneetra and Tawanna in her life, Natalie regretted sabotaging the friendship she'd had with Wendy. As she internalized Pastor Giles's sermon, she thought about the day she had seen Wendy at Babies "R" Us. The only reason she'd apologized then was because it was the right thing to do; she hadn't been sincere. Now she was doing it because it was the Christian thing to do—and because she was truly sorry for her acts of betrayal. Once again, she began writing:

Dear Wendy,

I hope all is well with you. A lot has transpired in my life since we last saw each other back in February at the store. For starters, I had a miscarriage and am no longer pregnant. The loss of my baby caused me finally to come to grips with my past, facing some things that had happened in my childhood, which I had allowed to harden me. The purpose of this letter is not to give you a sob story about my background. Rather, I really want to offer my deepest apologies for betraying you.

I remember you said that you'd already forgiven me. I want to thank you for that. I still feel it's necessary to admit my wrongdoing. I'm sure you could probably tell that my last apology wasn't sincere. I was still dealing with some issues back then and really hadn't come face to face with the horrible truth of what I did to you. Now, Wendy, I am sorry. I'm not saying this because I'm trying to be your best friend again. I realize it's very doubtful that my position as your friend will ever be restored. I just want to say thank you for always being a true friend to me. I'm sorry for betraying your trust. I pray that you will never be hurt again by a friend the way that I hurt you.

If I could go back in time, I would never hurt you again
Looking back, I now see that I lost a very good friend
Maybe one day our paths will cross then you'll be able to see
That the person who did those horrible things, was not the real me
I would have changed a long time ago if I had known what true friendship was all about
But I couldn't do it by myself; Jesus had to help me out

I'm sure you're probably asking yourself, "Can this really be?"
But deep down you know God can save anyone... including me
Thank you, Wendy, for forgiving me for all that I've done wrong
May His goodness and mercy follow you all the days long
Love,
Natalie

With tears blurring her vision, Natalie folded the letter and sealed it in an envelope.

Chapter 35

Super Cool

Natalie walked into her apartment and was greeted by the sound of the wind rushing against her window. Glad to be safely inside, away from the cold air, she put a pot of water on the stove for some hot cocoa. October was here already and once again Natalie was actively participating in the Breast Cancer Awareness campaign. She'd kept busy over the summer with work, church and some poetry workshops she'd been attending, thanks to Aneetra, who had encouraged her to pursue her talent.

While the water was working its way up to a boil, Natalie changed out of her work clothes into pajamas. *What a difference a year makes…*she thought. Last year, she'd delayed her plans to move back to New York because of Troy. This year, she'd completely abandoned the idea. Columbus was where she would remain unless the Lord led her otherwise.

Things were really going good for her. At last, she was at

peace and no longer tormented by the painful experiences of her past. She was still working on that whole forgiveness thing where Jesse was concerned, but, to her surprise, she no longer carried a sore spot about Sylvia and Richard's relationship, and she had been supportive of their recent engagement. She had even managed to cross her aunt off her list of transgressors.

"Coming!" she wanted to respond as the kettle whistled, as if doing so would silence the noise. Just as she slipped on her house shoes and rushed back into the kitchen, the phone started ringing. After turning off the stove, she raced back to her bedroom to answer it.

The 601 area code was definitely a Jackson telephone number, but the name A. Shepherd displayed on the caller ID threw her for a curve. "Hello?"

"Hi, Natalie. It's Toni."

She immediately feared the worse because the two of them hadn't said a single word to each other since their big blow-up. "What's wrong? Is Big Mama okay?"

"Yes, Mama is fine. I was hoping we could talk. Did I catch you at a bad time?"

"No…" Natalie sat on the edge of her bed. Her stomach churned. What could Toni possibly have to say to her that she hadn't said already?

"I called to apologize to you. I said some horrible things when you were down here and I want you to know that from the bottom of my heart I'm sorry."

"Thank you. I…accept your apology," she said in amazement.

"I also want you to know that I told Corrine who you really are."

"Seriously?" Excitement stirred in her spirit. "What changed your mind?"

"Besides the fact that God wouldn't allow me to have a lick

of peace until I did…I realized we both play an important role in Corrine's life. When she told me that she'd stopped hanging around with that LaShina girl, I got smug. Instead of commending her for being responsible and making a smart move, I fussed at her for not doing it sooner. I said that next time I try and tell her about one of her friends, she needed to listen to me immediately. I thought I was going to drop dead when she told me that you said some things which caused her to think about their friendship. Apparently, you had a much better and more effective way of delivering the same message. It was so silly of me to think I could keep the two of you away from each other forever. She told me all about the night you rescued her at the bar. If you hadn't been there…" The cracking of Toni's voice provided evidence of her tears. Natalie was starting to produce her own.

"I may not have known Corrine all of her life, but I do want what's best for her," she said.

"I know and I believe Corrine knows, too."

"So, how did she take it when you told her about me?"

"Quite well, actually. I told her several weeks ago and I made Mama promise not to say anything to you. I was trying to work up the nerve to call you myself. She knows everything. I feared telling her for so long because I was afraid she wouldn't be able to handle the truth, when all along it was me who couldn't handle it. I was scared of losing Corrine. I love her, and I guess the selfish part of me figured that if she knew you, there wouldn't be room enough in her life for the both of us."

"I would never try to replace you as Corrine's mama."

"I know. It was my own insecurity. When Corrine was growing up, there was no doubt in my mind that she and I wouldn't have the best relationship as she got older. Then she started going through the rebellious teenage years and I panicked. I remember not liking my mama and daddy too much during that time. The difference was I had no other options. There wasn't another mother I could go to if Mama got on my nerves. I was scared that I would fail Corrine somehow, and she would abandon me if she ever knew who her biological mother was."

"She recognizes everything you sacrificed to raise her. I can't see that ever happening."

"I know. Anyhow, I wanted you to know how truly sorry I am."

"I forgive you."

"Thanks, Natalie. Well, I'm going to let you go. Corrine's been sitting here and told me to ask if it would be okay to speak with you?"

"Of course it would be!" She was both nervous and excited at the same time.

"Hold on…"

Before Natalie could catch her next breath, Corrine was on the other end of the line. "Hi, Natalie." She sounded nervous also.

"Hey, how's it going?" Tears of joy trickled down her cheeks.

"I'm cool."

"Are you overwhelmed by the news of me being your birth mother?"

"No, not really. I mean, it sucks to know I'm a product of sexual abuse, but I'm glad to have answers finally. It's super cool to know that you're my birth mother. I mean, you are so pretty—not that my mama isn't. I used to try and picture what my biological mother would look like. I figured she was some prostitute or drug addict, and so I never imagined that she would be someone as beautiful as you."

"Thanks," Natalie said, not sure where the conversation was headed.

"That night when we were at the diner, after you dropped me off at the dorm, I thought, 'Man, she's real cool.' I mean, you sort of helped me out on the spot, like a big sister or something. Did you know who I was the night you saw me?"

"No. I had a feeling once we started talking and you told me about being adopted."

"Well, thanks again for looking out for me the way you did that night. I was hoping you'd be at Tawanna's wedding so I could tell you that."

"It's okay. I would do it again in a heartbeat."

Natalie listened intently as Corrine updated her on all the things that had taken place since they'd last seen each other. Big Mama had done a good job of keeping Natalie informed about Corrine, but Natalie so enjoyed the enthusiasm her daughter displayed that she pretended to be hearing the stories for the very first time. They stayed on the phone for well over an hour talking as though they'd known each other for years.

Chapter 36

Just for You

Easton Town Center was filled with holiday shoppers and Natalie was among them trying to wrap up her Christmas shopping. She wasn't used to having so many people on her list. She was going to Mississippi for Christmas and hadn't a clue what to get many of her family members, besides Corrine and Big Mama who were the first people she'd shopped for and also the ones she'd spent the most money on.

"Jingle bells, jingle bells, jingle all the way, oh what fun it is to ride in a one horse open sleigh…hey…" Natalie hummed along with the Christmas songs that played over the speakers. While some of the other shoppers grunted about how much money they were spending that season, she bounced as if she didn't have a care in the world. She was excited about spending time with her family this Christmas. If only her mother were still alive to see it.

The brisk, cold air forced Natalie to take a break from

shopping at the outside stores. She went inside Easton Station to buy a cup of hot chocolate, taking a seat at an empty table.

"Natalie?"

She looked up and saw Troy walking toward her. "Hey, how are you doing?"

"I'm good. How about yourself?" He greeted her with such a warm and attractive smile that she gladly returned one of her own.

"I'm doing good, too."

"Do you mind if I have a seat?"

"No, go right ahead."

"So what have you been up to?"

"Some of everything. Right now I'm just trying to finish up my Christmas shopping."

"Yeah, me, too. I'm going to Houston again."

"That should be nice. I'll be in Jackson."

"Going to visit your grandmother?"

"Mm-hmm."

"I hope you have a good time."

"Thanks, you, too."

"Um…I'm glad that I ran into you here. I've been thinking about you a lot…. I never did apologize for my behavior that last time we were together."

"It's okay. I'm not upset with you."

"There have been so many times I've thought about calling you, but I always chickened out. I didn't know how you would react."

"I wouldn't have been upset. In fact I tried e-mailing you one time. You never responded so I assumed you were still mad at me."

Troy looked surprised. "I don't remember getting an e-mail from you. I'm not saying that you didn't write me, I'm sure you did. For whatever reason, I don't remember.

I was probably too busy being bullheaded. I'm really sorry for everything."

"Thanks, Troy. I fully accept your apology. I promise that I have no hard feelings toward you."

"That's good to know…." He looked relieved. "Are you still going to church?"

"Yep. I have been ever since I came back from Mississippi."

"Good, glad to hear that." Troy's awkward smile caused Natalie to wonder what the true reason was behind his question. "So…what church do you attend?"

"Greater Grace. I officially became a member there about three weeks ago."

"Do you like it?"

"I *love* it. You remember my friend, Aneetra, from work don't you? She's the one you ca—"

"Yeah, yeah, I remember," he said playfully. "It sounds like God has placed you where you belong."

Wait a minute… Did he just say God? Her thoughts must've been readable from her facial expression because Troy spoke up.

"That probably sounded weird coming from me, didn't it?"

"I—I've never heard you talk like that before, that's all."

"That's because you and I have never held a conversation since I've been saved."

"*You're…saved?* By saved, you mean you've confessed your sins to Jesus, asked for forgiveness, and made Him Lord over your life?"

Troy laughed. "Yeees."

Natalie realized that she must've sounded really silly and laughed at herself. "Do you mind me asking what changed your mind about God and all?"

"I called my friend Elvin one night and shared my fears with him. He began to take me through the Bible, helping me understand some things. I can't recall all the scriptures he went over, but I know for a fact he concentrated very heavily on the book of Romans, going all through chapters five, six and ten. Thank God for the Internet because at the time I didn't even own a Bible. I pulled the scriptures up on my computer and read along with him. It was that night while we were on the phone Elvin led me in a prayer of repentance and I was saved."

Wow!

"Elvin had been talking to me for years and yet it wasn't until that day I started listening. Since then, I've been attending Fellowship Temple."

"Where's that at?"

"It's out west, in Hilliard. I'm not officially a member there. I've been going because I knew I needed to be someplace where I can learn and grow. Elvin and his wife were members of that church before they moved to Chicago. That's how I found out about it."

"That's great, Troy! I'm happy that things are coming together for you."

"Thanks…" He looked at Natalie as though he wanted to say something else, but didn't. "Well, I guess I should get back to shopping."

"Yeah, me, too. I've just got a few more things to get, then I'll be out."

"Lucky you. I'm just starting." He stood up and pushed his chair into the table. "It was good seeing you again."

"I feel the same way…"

"Will it be okay if I…um…called you sometime? You know, just to see how you're doing."

This was the first time during her encounter with Troy that Natalie felt a tickle in her stomach. She wanted to scream *Yes! Yes! Yes!* but settled on "No, I wouldn't mind at all," hoping her smile wasn't too big.

"Are your telephone numbers still the same?"

"Yes."

"Great! I guess I'll talk to you soon." Troy wished her a Merry Christmas and walked away.

Natalie waited until Troy was clear out of her sight before pulling out her cell phone. "Guess who I just saw?" she said to Aneetra.

Chapter 37

The Same Dilemma

"Girl, I think you should tell him," Aneetra urged.

Natalie had just got back in town from her trip to Mississippi. Troy had called her to wish her a Merry Christmas and asked if they could celebrate the first day of the New Year together on a date. With her cell phone pinned between her cheek and shoulder, and her mail from the last week shoved under her arm, she laid her luggage down so she could unlock the door to her apartment. "I don't know…maybe I need to wait to see how things are going to work out first."

"No, you do not!" Aneetra protested. "If you were going out with someone other than Troy tomorrow, I might agree with you. But you and Troy have a history together. It seems like part of the problem in your previous relationship is that both of you were scared to tell each other how you truly felt. Don't make the same mistake twice. You need to be honest with him upfront. The last thing you want to do is get involved with him again and then wait several months down the road to tell him about Corrine. He needs to know now."

Natalie began leafing through her mail. "I suppose you're right."

"I am. It's natural for you to be apprehensive, but don't let fear control you. Everything is going to be fine."

"Aneetra, let me call you back later," Natalie said when she saw a card among her mail with Wendy's name written in the return address.

"All right, girl. If I don't talk to you beforehand, I'll see you at Watch Night?

"Service is at ten, right?"

"Yeah, but I plan to be there by a quarter after nine so I can get a seat. A lot of folks come to church on New Year's Eve even if they don't come any other time."

"Okay. I'll try and meet you there at that time," Natalie hung up the phone and immediately opened the card. The outside of it had a picture of Baby Jesus in a manger and the words *Our Savior is Born* printed above it. The inside read: "Let's not forget that Jesus is the reason for the season. Let's celebrate Him this Christmas because without Him, we'd all be lost. Merry Christmas—Wendy." There was also a handwritten note that Natalie unfolded.

Dear Natalie,

I received the letter you'd written me some time ago. I must admit, I was quite surprised by your admission of guilt. First of all, I do forgive you. I also want to thank you for your sincere apology. Initially, I was a little skeptical, which is why it has taken me so long to respond, but after much prayer, I now believe you meant everything you wrote. Though I can't promise we'll ever be bosom buddies again, I also won't abandon the idea either. God has shown me that He's capable of

doing anything. Let's just take things one day at a time and see what happens. If our friendship is meant to be restored completely, God will work things out. Merry Christmas and I hope you have a happy New Year.
Love, Your Sister in Christ,
Wendy

Unbelievable! Natalie thought and refolded the letter. She wasn't going to try and push this friendship, recalling that Pastor Giles stated that healing takes time. After what Natalie had done to Wendy, it could only be by the grace of God that Wendy allowed herself to be open to the possibility of them being friends again. It confirmed to Natalie that God truly did have power to do what seemed impossible.

It was a few minutes after eight when Troy walked her inside to her apartment after they'd come back from seeing a movie. "Do you want to stay for a little while?" she asked. "I really would like to talk to you about something."

"Sure." Troy looked concerned, but took off his coat and followed Natalie to the couch. "What's up? I noticed you were sort of quiet tonight."

"Yes. Can I get you something to drink?"

"No. I'm fine, thank you. What would you like to talk to me about?" he pressed.

"Remember last year when you read that poem I wrote—the one you found on my desk?"

"Uh-huh."

"In it, I mentioned something about another baby. When I told you I had had a miscarriage, you asked me how long it had been since my previous one."

"I remember."

"Troy…I never had a miscarriage before the one I had last year."

"Okay. Did you have an abortion?"

Natalie shook her head no.

"I don't understand."

"I…I had a baby," she nervously admitted.

"A *baby?*" He was understandably shocked. "When?"

Natalie's heart raced as she shared her troubling childhood experience.

Compassion consumed Troy's expression. "You don't have to talk about this if you don't want to."

"No. It's okay. I don't want any secrets between us," she told him. Troy put his arm around her shoulders and Natalie leaned her head into his chest, hearing the rhythmic thump of his heart. "Last year when I went to Jackson, I found out that I'd had a daughter, and she'd been adopted by my aunt. Apparently, everyone knew this except for me—including my mom."

"She never told you?"

"No, she didn't, and that was really hard for me to come to grips with. I was mad at everyone, even my grandmother. It was crazy how I found out. My daughter knew she'd been adopted, but she didn't know I was her birth mother. Needless to say, things got really tense between my aunt and me. We got into this big argument—it was a mess. I didn't leave there on good terms with anyone."

"Wow…I probably made matters worse by acting like a jerk when you came back, huh?"

"I was scared to tell you because you flipped when I told you I was pregnant. I didn't know how you would respond if you knew I had a teenage daughter. At the time, she and I didn't have any contact because my aunt didn't want her to know who I was."

"I take it that the two of you have some kind of relationship now?"

"Yes, we do." Natalie answered, proudly.

"What's her name?"

"Corrine... She's nineteen."

"And she knows you're her birth mother?"

"Uh-huh."

"I really don't know what to say."

"Troy...Corrine *is* a part of my life now. Will you be able to accept that?"

He gently lifted Natalie's chin up so that she was inches from his face, looking him directly in the eyes. "Of course. Why would you think otherwise?"

"I don't know...it seems like I'm dropping some pretty big bombshells on you."

"Don't worry about it. I'm glad you felt comfortable enough to confide in me. I'm sorry that you've had to go through so much," he began to whisper. "But, I hope you'll give me a chance to be a part of whatever you have to go through from now on. I know I hurt you before, Natalie. I don't blame you for not wanting to trust me—so don't. Trust God and know that I'm trusting Him, too. Even if something happens that may be a little difficult for either of us to deal with immediately, we have Him to depend on."

Without saying anything else, Troy leaned down and, for the first time in months, Natalie felt the warm, soft, pleasure of his mouth against hers. It was a long kiss, growing in intensity each second, igniting the passion that had been dormant in her for a while.

"I'd better go," Troy whispered, his lips still dangerously close to hers.

"Why?" Natalie breathed.

"Because kissing you felt very good...*too* good, if I can be honest. Before we get ourselves caught up in something that'll be hard to stop, it'll be wiser if I leave now."

As much as she wanted him to stay, Troy had a point. That kiss had awakened some desires in her that wouldn't go back to sleep easily. "I think you're right," she smiled, giving him a quick peck before backing away from him and standing up. "I have to get up for work tomorrow anyhow."

"Yeah. Me, too." He and Natalie walked to the door hand-in-hand. "I'll call you tomorrow."

"I'll be waiting."

Troy grabbed her by the waist and leaned down to kiss her once again. Although shorter, the kiss was just as good—if not better—than the first one, and Natalie had to fight hard to keep thoughts from their previous sexual encounters from clouding her mind.

"I'd *really* better leave," Troy stated, letting go. He must've been in the same dilemma.

"Okay." Natalie took the initiative and opened the door. "Happy New Year."

"You, too." Natalie shut the door, leaned back, and smiled. *God, please don't take my desire for him away...but Lord, I need You to help me get it under control!*

Chapter 38

Proverbs 18:22

Troy nervously paced the floor of his living room as he waited for Natalie to show up. He couldn't recall a time in his life when he'd been this anxious about anything. He'd spent the entire day planning and hoping this Valentine's Day celebration would be one to remember.

He and Natalie had been dating each other since the first of the year. Troy couldn't get over how much their relationship had grown. The first time they were together, neither of them had been saved. Natalie was emotionally unstable and Troy had not yet come to terms with the problems of his upbringing. This time around they had a spiritual connection which brought peace and bonded them in a way they never had been before. Natalie had an inner beauty that greatly superseded her outer appearance—though Troy still found her attractive physically. What man wouldn't? She had all the right curves in all the right places.

Both he and Natalie had agreed that sexual intimacy was not an option for them, but that area was still a personal struggle for Troy. He'd explored her curvaceousness in their previous relationship so he knew that everything not only looked good, but felt good as well, thus, he often found himself fleeing whenever the atmosphere between them got heated.

Troy looked at his watch. It was six-fifteen. Natalie should be arriving any minute now. Walking back and forth was driving him crazy. Troy took several deep breaths, sat down on the couch and waited.

Natalie parked her car outside Troy's apartment building, got out and shook out any wrinkles that might have formed on her chocolate-colored pant suit on the way over. She hoped Troy would like the outfit. She'd bought it recently and it was sexy but elegant, complementing her figure nicely without provoking temptation by overexposing any of her physical attributes. Grabbing Troy's present from the back seat, Natalie walked up to the building and rang the intercom to Troy's apartment.

"Natalie, is that you?" He called out.

"Naw…who else did you invite over for a candlelight dinner?"

Troy was standing at the door waiting. "Hey there," she stopped to give him a gentle peck on the lips then walked past him into the apartment. "This is for you." She handed him his present.

"Thanks," he said, laying it on the counter. "Here, let me help you with your coat…. You look very nice."

"Thank you. So do you," she replied, "but you never answered my question."

"What was that?"

"I asked who else you had invited over for a candlelight dinner."

"Oh, nobody." He seemed not to notice that she was teasing. "Why don't you have a seat? I'll go ahead and get the food out of the oven and put it on the table."

From where Natalie sat, she was able to observe Troy's actions. He seemed to be preoccupied with something, nervously arranging and rearranging things on the table. He was really acting weird and Natalie wondered if something was wrong. However, she was impressed that Troy had ordered a catered meal for them. Originally, he'd mentioned taking her to Skyler's, but Natalie had admitted to him why she was no longer welcome there, telling him the whole ugly truth about what she had done to Wendy. Troy laughed and asked if there were any other restaurants in Columbus she was barred from attending. She'd thought he was making reservations at another restaurant until yesterday, when he'd asked if she would meet him here.

"I'm almost ready," he announced, inserting a jazz CD into the stereo and dimming the lights. "Okay, everything's all set," he said, coming over to Natalie and escorting her to the table.

"Are you all right?"

"Yeah, why? Are you?"

"Yes, Troy, but you are acting really strange."

"I am?"

"Yes, you are."

"I'm sorry, I don't mean to."

Natalie knew something was going on with him, but apparently he wasn't going to tell her what. She looked down at her plate of broiled lobster tails, rice and mixed vegetables. "This looks really nice."

"Before we say grace and eat, I want to give you something." Troy pulled a card from under his plate and held it out to her.

"Wait, let me get your present also." She started to get up.

"No, open this first, please," he insisted.

Natalie took the card and did as he wished. The words *I Love You* were printed inside a heart on the front. There were no preprinted messages on the inside, but a handwritten scripture from Proverbs 18:22 about a man finding a wife. At the end were the words "Happy Valentine's Day, Love, Troy."

"I don't understand…"

Troy got up from his side of the table and walked around to Natalie, bending on one knee. He reached inside his pocket, pulling out and opening a small box, which contained a large platinum solitaire.

"Oh my goodness!" She looked into Troy's teary eyes with her own.

"Natalie…" he began to speak with a shaky voice. "I love you. Will you do me the honor of becoming my wife?"

Chapter 39

Metamorphosis

Natalie and Troy were married that summer in a small ceremony at Greater Grace—the church they now both belonged to. Their families came from out of state to witness their nuptials. Natalie's grandmother represented the mother of the bride and her uncle Earl walked her down the aisle while her uncle Tommy was one of Troy's groomsmen. With Corrine as her maid of honor joined by bridesmaids Tawanna, Aneetra, Toni and Troy's sister, Natalie vowed to spend the rest of her life being Mrs. Troy Jermaine Evans.

A few months shy of their second wedding anniversary, Natalie and Troy were in Mississippi at Corrine's graduation ceremony. "And next we have Corrine Shepherd. Corrine is graduating summa cum laude with a degree in Marketing," the presenter announced as Corrine walked across the stage to receive her degree. Her entire family exploded in an uproar, standing to applaud and cheer her on. Both Natalie and Toni smiled adoringly as they watched Corrine pose so that Kenny and Troy could each take pictures.

Natalie's tall, round frame wobbled its way back into the seat as the expectant mother continued clapping. At eight months pregnant, she definitely wasn't displaying the hourglass figure she'd been used to. She was going to have to work hard to get back in shape after the baby was born. Even if she never fully recovered her figure, she was just glad that God had given her another chance to bring life into the world.

Natalie and Corrine had become as close as any birth mother and daughter could be. They talked every day. Soon they'd have a chance to spend time together on a daily basis over the summer because Corrine was planning to fly back with her and Troy. It was a visit that Troy, Natalie and Corrine were all looking forward to.

Feeling a jolt inside her, Natalie rubbed her belly. Troy must've witnessed this because he leaned over and asked, "Are you okay?"

Natalie smiled, flattered by his concern, and said, "I'm fine."

Troy reached into her lap and gently squeezed her hand. "I love you," he mouthed.

"I love you, too," she mimicked to him.

Sometimes she pinched herself to make sure she wasn't dreaming. God had certainly been good to her and she knew she'd done nothing to deserve His love or favor. God had turned her whole life around and she was so grateful, gladly sharing her faith with others. Having continued with her poetry writing, she revised the poem that Troy had found on her desk the night he'd received her goodbye letter. At the time it had been called "My Secrets," but she'd renamed it "Metamorphosis" because she wanted it to reflect what had taken place in her life after she'd turned it over to Jesus. If it had not been for the Lord by her side, she wasn't sure where she'd be, but she was sure that she'd be in a mess.

When I looked in the mirror, what did I see? Someone who didn't like to look back at me.

I closed my eyes so very fast; I opened them back up and saw my past.

If only I could've turned back the hands of time, I would've fixed those things that weighed on my mind.

Taking a trip down memory lane, I saw things I did that I now think are insane.

There was a man who had been my first. That experience was by far my worst.

I was so young and very naïve, he planted the seed and I conceived.

What age you ask? I may never reveal; It's between God and me, my lips are sealed.

After the other was gone, I didn't know what to do. A little voice suggested popping a pill or two.

I must admit that I was very close to riding on the freeway of overdose,

But I got scared and began to cry, I didn't know if I was really ready to die.

But wait…since then I have changed. No longer the same person, I just carry the same name.

The outside is similar but the inside is not; God came in and erased every spot.

Now when I look through God's eyes, what do I see? Someone who truly loves the God in me.

Despite what I've done in the past, I've found peace that is sure to last.

His grace and love have made me brand-new. What He's done for me, He can do for you.

Therefore if any man be in Christ, he is a new creature: old things are passed away; behold, all things are become new.
(2 Corinthians 5:17)

Book Discussion Questions

1. Though Natalie had deceived Kevin for months, do you think he responded properly at the restaurant? Why or why not?

2. What's your relationship with your earthly father? What's your relationship with your Heavenly Father? Do you think a person's relationship with his/her earthly father sometimes has a bearing on how he/she might relate to his/her Heavenly Father?

3. Is there at least one person in your life you can turn to for spiritual support? What are some benefits of having godly influences?

4. Ida Mae warns Natalie about the dangers of having a negative attitude. Proverbs 18:21 states that the power of life and death are in our tongue. Think of a time in your life where your words affected the outcome of a situation—either for good or for bad.

5. Do you think it's pride or low self-esteem that prompts a woman to use her body to get ahead in life? Could it be a combination of both? If neither, what would you say it is?

6. Does Natalie have a right to be upset with Sylvia and/or Richard? Why or why not? Ephesians 4:26 says to "Be angry and sin not…." In what ways did Natalie violate this biblical instruction? In what ways have you violated it?

7. Ida Mae states that Psalm is one of her favorite books in

the Bible. Do you have a favorite? What is it and why is it your favorite?

8. Immediately Natalie is physically attracted to Troy. What initially attracted you to your spouse or significant other? Was it his/her looks or another attribute?

9. Because of meeting Troy, Natalie has changed her initial plan of moving back to New York. Do you think this was a wise decision? What are some dangers of basing life decisions on a relationship—especially one that is fairly new?

10. How would you have handled Natalie if you were in Wendy's place? Do you think Wendy's response was Christ-like? Why or why not?

11. Troy uses his job as an excuse for not wanting to start a family. To what degree does your work interfere with your family life?

12. Natalie thinks she can change Troy's mind about their situation by seducing him. Why do you think she feels so desperate to keep Troy in her life?

13. Troy thinks Natalie is just playing a game with him. What games do women and men play in relationships as a way to exert control?

14. Have you ever lost touch with a loved one? What actions did you take to find him/her?

15. Natalie is still haunted by unfortunate events from her childhood. What negative experiences from your child-

hood still bother you today? Are you taking steps to resolve these unsettled issues? What are they?

16. Natalie doesn't think she needs God for her problems. Why do you think many people acknowledge God exists, but refuse to acknowledge the need for Him in their own lives?

17. Natalie is very discouraged in Chapter 24. If you could offer her advice at this point what would it be?

18. It appears that Natalie is once again trying to run from her problems in Chapter 24. What kinds of activities do you engage in that prevent you from dealing with your problems head-on?

19. Do you (or have you ever) feared getting married or having children? How have your childhood experiences influenced your views of marriage and parenting—positively or negatively?

20. If you're a Christian, think back to the time when you first gave your life to Christ. What events led up to this decision? In retrospect, can you see ways God was trying to get your attention before then?

21. Natalie thinks about Proverbs 3:5, which states "Trust in the Lord with all thine heart and lean not unto thine own understanding." When going through storms, are you able to apply this scripture to your own life?

22. Do you think Natalie was right to confront Toni? Why or why not? Does the Bible give instructions on how to handle conflict with fellow Christians?

23. Natalie learns that forgiveness is a necessary component of her Christian walk. What are some barriers that prevent us from forgiving? What advice would you give someone who is having difficulty applying forgiveness to a particular person? Is immediate forgiveness really possible? Why or why not?

24. Why do you think Natalie felt comfortable enough to share her secret with Aneetra when she hadn't shared it with anyone else, including Wendy?

25. Some people believe that all religions ultimately lead to the same God—even if we don't all have the same beliefs. If you're a Christian and you believe this, how do you justify this belief considering Jesus' words in 1 John 14:6?

26. One of the signs of a mature Christian is someone who can admit wrongdoing. Tell about a time when you had to apologize to someone for hurting them—even though you may have done so unintentionally.

27. Are you a single (i.e., unmarried) Christian? What measures do you and your boyfriend/girlfriend take to prevent falling into sexual temptation with each other?

28. Compare Natalie's character in *Soul Matters* and now. What does this say about the power of God to change lives?

Three powerful stories of
mothers, daughters, faith
and forgiveness.

BESTSELLING AUTHORS

STACY HAWKINS ADAMS
KENDRA NORMAN-BELLAMY
LINDA HUDSON-SMITH

This Far by *Faith*

The relationships between three women and their
mothers are explored in this inspirational anthology.
As secrets and lies are brought to light, each must
learn about redeeming faith, the power of
forgiveness and enduring love.

*Coming the first week of April
wherever books are sold.*

NEW SPIRIT

™

www.kimanipress.com

KPANTHOL0240408TR

The inspirational sequel to

He's **FINE**...*But Is He* **SAVED?**

Acclaimed author

KIMBERLEY BROOKS

He's

SAVED...

But Is He

FOR

REAL?

An entertaining novel about men, dating, relationships and God.

Sandy, Michelle and Liz are three single girlfriends who are each struggling with their own issues with men. As each faces confusion, jealousy and loneliness, they look to the one Lord and Savior of all for help.

"Heartwarming and engrossing...
He's Fine...But Is He Saved?
engages you from the first page to the last."
—Bestselling author Jacquelin Thomas

Coming the first week of February wherever books are sold.

Because even the smartest women can make
relationship mistakes...

ACCLAIMED AUTHOR
JEWEL DIAMOND TAYLOR

You DESERVE MORE

A straight-to-the point book that will empower women
and help them overcome such self-defeating emotions as
insecurity, desperation, jealousy, loneliness...all factors that
can keep you in a destructive cycle of unloving, unfulfilling
relationships. Through the powerful insights and life-lessons
in this book, you will learn to build a relationship that's
strong enough to last a lifetime.

"Jewel Diamond Taylor captivates audiences. She moves the spirit."
—Susan L. Taylor, Editorial Director, *Essence* magazine

Available the first week of January, wherever books are sold.

NEW SPIRIT
™

www.kimanipress.com

A volume of heartwarming devotionals
that will nourish your soul...

NORMA DeSHIELDS BROWN

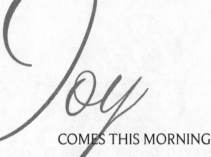

Joy

COMES THIS MORNING

Norma DeShields Brown's life suddenly changed
when her only son was tragically taken from her
by a senseless act. Consumed by grief, she began
an intimate journey that became
Joy Comes This Morning.

Filled with thoughtful devotions, Scripture readings
and words of encouragement, this powerful book
will guide you on a spiritual journey that will sustain
you throughout the years.

*Available the first week of November
wherever books are sold.*

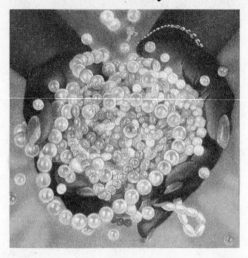